RAISING
SELF-ESTEEM IN
PRIMARY SCHOOLS

A WHOLE SCHOOL TRAINING PROGRAMME

Margaret Collins

SAGE

Los Angeles | London | New Delhi
Singapore | Washington DC

First published 2009

SAGE Publications
1 Oliver's Yard
55 City Road
London EC1Y 1SP

SAGE Publications Inc.
2455 Teller Road
Thousand Oaks, California 91320

SAGE Publications India Pvt Ltd
B 1/I 1 Mohan Cooperative Industrial Area
Mathura Road, Post Bag 7
New Delhi 110 044

SAGE Publications Asia-Pacific Pte Ltd
33 Pekin Street #02-01
Far East Square
Singapore 048763

Illustrator: Philippa Drakeford

Library of Congress Control Number 2009921353

British Library Cataloguing in Publication data
A catalogue record for this book is available from the British Library

ISBN 978-1-84860-775-0 (pbk)
ISBN 978-1-84920-069-1 (hb)

Typeset by C&M Digitals (P) Ltd, Chennai, India
Printed on paper from sustainable resources
Printed in India at Replika Press Pvt Ltd.

THE UNIVERSITY OF
WINCHESTER

Martial Rose Library
Tel: 01962 827306

Check for
CD-Rom

SE
PR

- 9 OCT 2012

- 5 APR 2013

2 4 MAY 2013

2 4 OCT 2013

2 2 MAY 2014

7/5/14

22nd May

S

To be returned on or before the day marked above, subject to recall.

About the author

Margaret Collins, a mature student, trained as a teacher in Manchester after working in other situations. She taught infant and junior children in Lancashire, Kent, Surrey and Hampshire becoming first deputy head and later head of an infant school with army children in Aldershot. Later she became head of a first school in Cowplain, Hants.

Following early retirement, Margaret became a Visiting Fellow at Southampton University where she worked with the late Noreen Wetton, using the Draw and Write research technique to obtain children's responses on a number of health topics and co writing books with her. In 1991 Margaret started to write articles mainly on PSHE for journals for the early years. Her first book was a collaboration with Noreen for the Metropolitan Police *Who can help Andy?* In 1995 her first solo book, *Keeping Safe* was published by Forbes. This has been followed by 24 books for primary teachers, mainly published by Luck Duck Publishing.

Margaret works in schools designing 'Draw and Write' scenarios to collect children's responses mainly on health topics, analysing their responses and producing reports. The most recent one in 2008 is not on a health topic but on reading for a group of schools in West Sussex.

She also talks about her work and runs occasional training sessions for teachers and early years practitioners.

Contents

Introduction

Many people have low self-esteem; it affects the way they view the world. Challenges become worrying obstacles, learning new skills becomes so difficult that they give up before they try. They feel inferior, no good, and stop trying. It is the same with children.

The 'Every Child Matters' programme lists five aims. These are to enable children to:

- be healthy
- stay safe
- enjoy and achieve
- make a positive contribution
- achieve economic wellbeing.

Children with low self-esteem will not find this easy. They will have difficulty in partaking in classroom lessons and succeeding. Their low self-esteem will hold them back and they will come to expect failure. If we want to help children in the primary school to achieve these aims it is necessary to raise children's self-esteem.

Our self-esteem develops and evolves throughout our lives as we build an image of ourselves through what we do and what we experience. Experiences, particularly during childhood play a large role in the shaping of our basic self-esteem. How we are treated by the members of our immediate family, by teachers, children and other adults all contribute to the formation of basic self-esteem.

Many children have low self-esteem. It is not surprising that they feel small in the complex and important world of adults. They are still learning to do so many things and their mistakes are often treated with dismay and put down to them being 'only a child'. Well meaning adults use phrases such as 'you stupid thing', 'that's wrong', or 'you ought to be able to do that by now' so often that it is no wonder that many children begin to feel inferior.

Some parents (and teachers) even try to shame children into doing things that frighten them. Rosie, a seven year old, in *Not all Tarts are Apples*[1] says:

> ... neither Uncle Bert nor Auntie Maggie were of the persuasion that the way to encourage a frightened kid was to jeer at it, in public or private. Some parents do that, don't they – shame children into doing things that terrify them? I remember being really shocked the first time I saw someone do that to their child. Even I squirmed with humiliation.

[1] Granger, Pip (2002) *Not all Tarts are Apples*, Bantam Press, page 171.

Promoting Children's Mental Health within Early Years and School Settings, DfEE 2001.

Mental health is about maintaining a good level of personal and social functioning. For children and young people, this means:

getting on with others, both peers and adults

participating in educative and other social activities

having a positive self-esteem. (p. iv)

On page 1 it states that children who are mentally healthy have been defined as:

having the ability to initiate, develop and sustain mutually satisfying personal relationships' and 'become aware of others and empathise with them.

Raising the self-esteem of the children we teach in school can only be a good thing. If we can encourage them to feel confident, successful and able to tackle new tasks they may begin to see the world as a place of wonder and adventure; a place where they feel confident to learn.

We can help children with poor self-esteem by giving them positive experiences and success which will help them to put aside any negative feelings about themselves. We must help them to accept themselves as they are, help them to acknowledge their strengths and limitations and still accept themselves as worthwhile beings. We can help to increase their self-esteem if we:

- encourage them to make choices, thus fostering independence in children
- thank them whenever they do something good and give lots of praise
- listen to their opinions with interest and enthusiasm, showing we value these opinions
- take the time to explain reasons
- encourage them to try new and challenging activities.

Self-concept

Self-concept is our awareness of our own characteristics. A baby has no self-image; it is formed at home as he grows. When a child starts school or pre-school s/he experiences other things for the first time and receives feedback from others outside the family. The child looks at how these other people see him, interprets and reflects on these impressions as his own his self-image is continually being reformed.

Ideal self

As the child's self-image is developing s/he comes to understand that there are ideal characteristics s/he should possess; that there are ideal standards of behaviour, skills and attitudes which are valued. This process begins at home, fostered by the family, and continues at pre-school or school as the child compares him/herself with those s/he meets there. The young child sees these ideal images around him/her and strives to some degree to attain them.

Self-esteem

Self-esteem is the child's personal evaluation of his/herself; the difference between the self-image and the ideal self.

Some children, particularly those with high self-esteem, aspire to reach the ideal self, working towards improving themselves, their behaviour, attitudes and skills. Others, especially those with low self-esteem, find difficulty in achieving these aspirations and fail to move towards the ideal self.

Our self-concept embraces all the attitudes and beliefs that we hold about ourselves. This self-concept is linked to our self-image; how we perceive ourselves is based on how others see us. Our ideal self is a picture of ourselves as how we would like to be; the characteristics and behaviour we would like to possess. Our self-esteem is a personal evaluation of our self; this is the difference between our self-image and our ideal self.

Therefore a child's self-esteem is based on what other people think and say about him, how he feels, how he is valued. How you view each child is important; value him and he will value himself; undervalue him and he will do the same. Find his good points and praise them and he will feel good about himself; point out his poor points and he will be convinced that he is worthless.

Self-esteem is therefore circular:

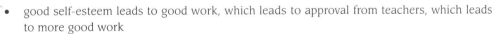

* good self-esteem leads to good work, which leads to approval from teachers, which leads to more good work
* poor self-esteem leads to poor work, which leads to disapproval from teachers, which leads to even more poor work.

Where there is a negative circle we need to break it and get children into a positive one. As adults we tend to do the things we are good at and avoid the things we are bad at. In schools, we often find the things that children can't do, for example, read – and make them do more of it! No sooner have they reached a target than we push them on to the next. They rarely have time to celebrate their achievement before we move on. Is this really desirable? Could this not, in fact, be lowering self-esteem? It is really important to set achievable goals, praise the achievement and celebrate it well before moving on to new and more challenging tasks.

The *National Curriculum Handbook*, in its non-statutory guidelines for PSHE on page 136 suggests that activities and experiences across the curriculum will enable children to:

* recognise their own worth
* learn to co-operate

- become responsible for their own learning
- understand their personal and social development
- explore spiritual, moral, social and cultural issues
- respect common humanity diversity and difference
- recognise the importance of forming effective and fulfilling relationships so essential to life.

The National Curriculum states that teachers help children to:

develop relationships through work and play, for example, by taking part in activities with groups that have particular needs, such as children with special needs and the elderly; communicating with children in other countries by computer links, e-mail or letters

take responsibility, for example in planning, and looking after the school environment; for the needs of others, such as by acting as a peer supporter, as a befriender, or as a playground mediator for younger pupils; for looking after animals properly; for identifying safe, healthy and sustainable means of travel when planning their journey to school

feel positive about themselves, for example, by producing personal diaries, profiles and portfolios of achievements; by having opportunities to show what they can do and how much responsibility they can take.

While most people agree that raising each child's self-esteem is a good thing, it is not always easy to achieve. How do we measure how we feel about ourselves unless it is a reflection of how we think other people see us? The old notion about giving a child ten praises for each censure is still important to do, even though it can be difficult to find things to praise some children for. If we really want to improve the self-esteem of children in our class or school we need to find something to praise; even if we need to manufacture it! When they fall by the wayside we need to use encouraging and understanding ploys to stop their self-esteem from plummeting. And it's no good leaving all that to the teachers; building good self-esteem will fall by the wayside if ancillary staff, learning assistants, school meals assistants and other adults are not included. We also need to get parents involved. If we want to help children to feel good about being at school and good about learning we need a whole school programme.

Raising the self-esteem of the adults who work in primary schools is also something to work towards. The workshops in this programme will go a long way to ensuring that all adults feel cared for, wanted and valued for themselves and for their work in schools.

A whole school programme

Adults' and children's self-esteem will be enhanced when they are treated seriously and with respect; treated as intelligent individuals, able to understand and reach conclusions. As an adult we want to be treated like this and children are no different. Anyone, adult or child, who is belittled, patronized or put down will suffer a lack of confidence. Mutual respect will foster trust and confidence.

Everyone fails at times but when we do fail we should not feel that we are 'a failure'. Can we teach children that failure doesn't exist; that there will be temporary setbacks on the road to success and that he hasn't succeeded **yet**? Telling a child that he has failed or let you down is counterproductive. We must try to help children to believe in his or her ability to succeed no matter how long it takes.

If your school is to embark on a programme of raising self-esteem in children it must be emphasised that this is not only a task for teachers. Everyone in the school has to be committed to the notion that raising self-esteem is not only a good thing; it is also essential for the wellbeing of adults and children alike. How we treat each other, how we interact, our body language as well as the words we use are important. Children learn by imitation; if they see an adult behaving badly towards another adult it will seem acceptable behaviour. Tone of voice, body language are both important, as well as conveying a sense of inclusion and tolerance to all.

This book seeks to give adults in schools tools to look at the way they could enhance self-esteem in children. There are inset sessions for adults, at the end of which everyone in school will have had time to appraise how they interact with children; how they use praise; how they use ways to raise self-esteem in order to make children feel good about themselves and their work, which will in turn raise the standard of learning in the children themselves. Some inset sessions are for all adults in the school; some for non-teaching personnel; some for teachers and classroom assistants.

As well as the in-service training for adults there are classroom lessons and activity sheets for the children. These can form part of your school's personal, social and health education (PSHE) programme. Some of these lessons are an integral part of the in-service training; others are for further work after the in-service training has been completed and before an evaluation of the effectiveness of the programme. There is also a place for the children's voice, which should take place before starting this programme. It will help you to find out the children's feelings about coming to school; where they feel comfortable and confident and where they do not.

This book, therefore, has five main sections:

1. Am I confident? A strategy for obtaining an insight into how children feel about coming to your school
2. Adult training sessions for mid-day supervisors (MDSs) and other adults working in school
3. Adult training sessions for teachers and classroom assistants
4. Lessons and activity sheets for the children as an integral part of the adult training
5. Further lessons and activity sheets for children as an ongoing part of their personal and social learning.

The Appendix contains:

- A useful self-esteem profile page at the end which could be used with older children as a check sheet
- The optimist creed
- Resources.

Summary of contents

Section 1 The Draw and Write classroom based illuminative research
strategy: 'Am I confident?'
This is a Draw and Write research strategy to use with each class of children
to try to obtain from them their feelings about school and any worries and concerns they
might have.

There are comprehensive instructions so that a class teacher can do this with the whole
class at one sitting and it should take 20 to 30 minutes. For classes where young children
are still struggling to write for themselves it would be useful to have your classroom
assistant and anyone else available to scribe for the children. These people should
write only what the child dictates and not question them about what they say, even
if it does not seem to make sense. Teachers of the youngest children may like to do
this research strategy in two separate sessions.

This strategy should be done before any of the self-esteem work takes place in order to
find out how the children feel before the start of the programme. This will provide
baseline data. The strategy can then be repeated at the end of the programme. By
comparing the difference in the children's responses, an evaluation of the success of
your teaching will be obtained.

Section 2 Training workshops for mid-day supervisors (MDSs) and other adults
You may like to include other adults in some of the workshops; perhaps new classroom
assistants or parents who help in school or others who come into contact with the children.

After a general introduction there are 8 sessions:

- a short pre-training session for other adults as well as MDSs
- a Circle Time session with children and teacher for other adults as well as MDSs
- Workshops 1–3, suitable for other adults as well as MDSs
- Workshops 4–6, mainly for MDSs.

Section 3 Training workshops for teachers and classroom assistants
There are seven training sessions for teachers and others who work closely with the
children in the classrooms. The first one relates to the children's Draw and Write
response sheets, the second starts with a presentation about self-esteem. The
remaining five include the first five topics for children.

Section 4 Lessons and activity sheets for children: an integral part of the adult training
These are in the form of five lessons each with an activity sheet for each of the three
age groups (5–7, 8–9, 10–11) and are integral to the self-esteem programme.

Section 5 Five further lessons and activity sheets
It is suggested that these are used as part of the normal PSHE programme. Some
schools may like to follow up these lessons with teacher discussions.

Classroom lessons and activity sheets

There are three sets of classroom activities for each topic, in three different age groups. Though age groups have been suggested, you may prefer to mix and match between the age groups to find work that is suitable for the children you teach. Each page of activities has an activity sheet. If you want to involve parents in enhancing children's self-esteem encourage children to take home their activity sheet.

These activity sheets are an integral part of each lesson and are arranged on facing pages with the youngest age group first followed by the later age groups. Activity sheets for the 5–7 year olds have a wordbox of suggestions to help children to complete the sheet. Children may choose not to use these words and there is space for teachers to add words that the child requests. Teachers are advised to look at the lessons and activity sheets for all three age groups to determine which is more suitable for their class. Some teachers may like to use ideas from activity sheets for a different age group to incorporate into their lesson. These lessons and activity sheets are also useful for children with learning difficulties if the appropriate level is selected and the child works alongside a learning support teacher.

See 'How to use this book' for more about activity sheets.

The following topics are covered in this book:

topics	5–7 year olds	8–9 year olds	10–11 year olds
being positive	the bright side being an optimist	positive thinking turns out for the best	challenges half empty/half full
same, different and special	same and different all special	different talents what makes me special?	good points special gifts
feeling good	feeling good at school what makes us feel good?	skills confidence	valuing achievements enjoyment
communication	listening and speaking body language	presentation how I say it	what do I mean? speaking out
praise and rewards	praise me rewards for us	give and accept praise treating ourselves	taking pride celebrate
doing well	I am good at getting better	growing well learning well	working well working better
friendships	being a good friend what do I look for?	working with friends family friends	grown-up friends role models
joining in	I join in with friends I let others join in	working together playing together	including being welcomed
making choices	doing the right thing good persuasion	good choices difficult choices	healthy choices moral choices
feeling confident	co-operating in someone's shoes	assertiveness self belief	strengths control

How to use this book

There are various ways of using the book. It is suggested that those in charge of running the programme first consider how to best cover this in their particular school and make a timetable that fits in with their overall school improvement plan. They need to agree which term is most suitable for starting the programme (the autumn term would best) and set dates for the sessions that allow everyone sufficient time to do the work between the dates. This timetable should be agreed by the teachers and others in the school beforehand and everyone should have a copy.

This whole school programme could take place over one or two terms. Using the 'Am I confident?' Draw and Write research strategy with all the children prior to the work will give baseline data which could be compared with data from the same strategy being employed at the conclusion of the programme. In this way the children's response sheets can be used for evaluation with older children being encouraged to see how their perceptions have changed over time.

It is vital to involve the MDSs and other adults who work in the school in this work. The time they spend with the children needs to support the notion of self-esteem in your school being important; they need to realise that they have a very special role in this. Their involvement will make or mar the success of the programme.

- One option is to set up the workshops with the MDSs first, concentrate on these and discuss the outcomes as a whole staff as these are ongoing. The workshops for teachers and other adults could take place the following term or half term.
- You could set up the MDS workshops first and then run the teachers and other adults sessions alongside these.
- You could use the programme with one year group, although the impact of the programme will be lost if the whole school is not involved in the task of improving everyone's self-esteem at the same time.
- If an individual classroom teacher wishes to use the programme without the whole school being involved they could browse through it and select the parts that are particularly relevant to them, their children and their teaching, using just those sections.

The teachers' workshops rely on text from the PowerPoint presentation. The text from each slide is in the preparation box for each session so that those who prefer not to use PowerPoint can write the text on a flipchart or an OHP transparency.

Activity sheets
This programme relies heavily on a school based approach to supporting self-esteem through classroom lessons with an activity sheet to reinforce each lesson.

Activity sheets designed for three different age groups gives more choice for teachers; ideas from one age group can be used with other age groups, even at a different level Each age group of activity sheets has a different border to facilitate ease in selection.

A good activity sheet can be used as a lesson. The ideas on the activity sheets can be interpreted in ways that suit various children and could, instead, be used as stimulus for class lessons. For this reason the activity sheets are grouped together by topics and across the age ranges. As well as whole class reinforcement, the activity sheets can be used in the following ways:

- the youngest children or those with learning difficulties could work through the activity sheets individually or in small groups
- the activity sheet ideas could be used individually, with a learning support teacher by children with special needs without the need for children completing the actual sheets
- classroom assistants could write on the activity sheets for children who are unable to write for themselves or ask children to draw pictures that convey their responses
- older children could work in pairs or groups to complete the activity sheets.

The CD

Though pages from the book can be enlarged to A4 and photocopied, teachers will find it more convenient to use the CD for printing copies both of the training sessions and the activity sheets.

There is a PowerPoint presentation which can be used in the training sessions. The text from this is also in the book so that teachers who prefer not to use PowerPoint can make a copy on a flipchart or overhead projector.

On the CD you will find:

- The PowerPoint slides

- Section 1
  The complete instructions for the 'Am I confident?' Draw and Write research strategy, together with the children's response sheets and the data collection sheet which can either be printed off separately or used on a computer for the data collection.

- Section 2
  The six workshops for the MDSs
  Do's and Don't's for MDSs
  Resources list for MDSs

- Section 3
  The four OHP visuals for Session 1
  Session 1 the 'Am I confident?' responses
  Session 2 Why promote self-esteem?
  Session 3 What can we do?
  Session 4 Valuing ourselves
  Session 5 Communication
  Session 6 Praise and rewards
  Session 7 And finally…

- Section 4
  Grid showing the topics for this section
  The activity sheets that are integral to the teachers' sessions

- Section 5
  Grid showing the topics for this section
  The activity sheets to be used as part of the normal PSHE programme in school

- Appendix
  Suggested Certificate of attendance for MDSs
  Self-esteem profile
  The Optimist Creed

Section 1 The Draw and Write classroom based illuminative research strategy: 'Am I confident?'

The Draw and Write research strategy was originally devised by the late Noreen Wetton in 1979 as part of a Master's degree course option in the philosophy of language.

Draw and Write strategies provide insights into how the children themselves perceive and explain the world around them and how they feel about what they perceive.

It is an inclusive strategy. No child has to be excluded on the grounds of inability to read and write. Even if the child's drawing is nothing more than a few scribbled lines, the child, can add her/his own explanation and this can be dictated to a scribe. So Draw and Write becomes Draw and Talk. It is the telling and writing which can be analysed and from which data can be drawn.

Draw and Write is non-threatening, not only to the children, but to their families, as children do not put their name on the response sheet. The children are encouraged to write or dictate in response to a very open invitation in as much or as little detail as they wish. There is no compulsion to respond. Children are allowed to write nothing or 'I don't know.'

The importance of the strategy is the way in which the children see themselves as being consulted and their views and perceptions taken seriously and put to use.

It is suggested that teachers carry out this Draw and Write strategy with their class before the start of this programme using the instructions and response sheets on the following pages and on the CD. There will be a discussion of the findings in the first session of Section 3 training workshops for teachers and classroom assistants.

Am I confident?

The 'Am I confident?' Draw and Write research strategy has been designed specifically for this self-esteem programme.

General instructions for 'Am I Confident?'
Introduce the activity by telling the children that;

- your school wants to find out how confident they all feel about coming to school and learning
- they are going to be doing some special drawing and writing work
- there are no right or wrong answers
- everything they draw or write will be useful
- they must not put their name on this paper as this work is anonymous
- only teachers will see these papers, so children can write what they feel.

There are only two rules for this work. They are:

- draw and write about how you feel – not about how you think you should feel
- don't share your work with, or talk about it to, anyone else while you are working.

Explain that you are all going to work at the same time on this work. You will ask them to start by drawing a picture and that when everyone has got started, you will ask them to stop their drawing and do some writing. When they have finished their writing they can go back and finish their picture. You will tell everyone when to stop and move on to the next box and when you do this, they must all stop what they are doing and listen to the instructions for the next part so that they don't get left behind.

Assure them that after the session you will give time for them to talk as a group about anything they would like to discuss.

Response sheets
Duplicate the response sheets; one double-sided sheet for each child.

Give each child a response sheet; ask them to write at the top of the paper the date and the name of their class and to write B or G in the box to show whether they are boy or girl. Explain to young children that the boxes for their responses are numbered and that they should start at Box 1.

With young children you may like to do this research activity on two separate occasions. It is not necessary for the children to write both parts on the same paper; if you do this, you will need to repeat the instructions carefully for the second part and ensure that children complete the date, year group and gender boxes on their second response sheet.

Demonstrate where to start by showing young children Box 1.

The 'Am I confident?' Draw and Write research strategy

Box 1
Draw yourself at school on a day when you feel good about being here.

Box 2
Write what makes you feel good about being at school.

Box 3
Draw yourself at school on a day when you feel not so good about being here.

Box 4

1. Write what makes you feel not so good about being here.
2. Who can help?

Box 5
Draw pictures of some of the places where you feel safe and happy here at school.

Box 6

Write why you feel safe and happy in these places.

Box 7

Draw pictures of any places where you do not feel safe and happy here at school.

Box 8

1. Write the names of these places and write why you don't feel happy and safe there.
2. Who can help?

Ask the children to place their paper, the right way round, in a pile for girls and a pile for boys.

Allow time for discussion

Analysis or data collection

In order to compare the 'before' and 'after' responses, you may like to read through them and note any of interest and any that cause concern. Alternatively you may like to use the data collection sheet to collect the data which will make later comparisons easier.

Class name............................. Age...................... B or G

Box 1	Box 2

Box 3	Box 4
	1. 2.

Class name............................ Age...................... B or G

Box 5	**Box 6**

Box 7	**Box 8** 1. 2.

code	2. happy child	4. not happy child	4. who?	6. good places	8. not good places	8. who?	comments
	smiley face	sad face	named person	smiley face	sad face	named person	
	home circumstance	home circumstance	teacher	warm	cold	teacher	
	positive feelings	ill, sick	child	comfortable	dark	child	
	good teacher	negative feelings		safe	named places		
	supportive friends	unhelpful teacher		good friends	no/poor friends		
	appropriate work	no, poor friends		supportive teachers	other children		
	good play	difficult work		other adults	bullying		
	interesting resources	unhappy play			no adult supervision		
		no, poor resources					
		personal worries					

What have you discovered?

The data generated by the children will give you, as the class teacher, some idea as to how your children feel about coming to school.

The data will inform you of:

- how many children drew smiling faces that show they feel confident
- how many made positive statements about coming to school
- what about your classroom or school makes children feel confident learners
- how many children drew sad faces
- whether they had negative feelings or don't feel confident about school
- people who can help them when things are not going well
- places where they feel comfortable and safe
- people with whom they feel confident and safe
- places where they feel uncomfortable or unsafe
- why they feel like this
- people they trust to help them if they have problems.

Read through the children's response sheets. This will give a clear picture of how confident children are in your class and school and point to whether they have high or low self-esteem. You may like to write some of the children's comments in speech bubbles to make a wall display about the children's positive feelings about being in your class and coming to your school.

If you wish to collect data on the data collection sheet, separate boys' and girls' response sheets so that you can note any interesting variations between the genders. It will be necessary to give each child's response sheet a code number. Write the code number on the sheet and put the figure 1 in each column where the child has made a response. Totalling up these figures will give an overall picture of the class response as a whole and whether there are any gender variations. You could to print off the data collection sheet, or use the one on the CD and complete it on a computer.

If every class in the school takes part in this research and collects numerical data it will give a clear picture right across the school and provide a basis for discussion about where there are problem areas which need to be addressed. This discussion will form part of the first teachers' workshop.

Evaluation

After the teachers' sessions and the first five topics you can repeat the 'Am I confident?' research strategy. Collect the children's responses and compare these with those obtained before the self-esteem work. If you collect numerical data you can easily compare the figures within each class and with the school as a whole. If you prefer not to collect numerical data, reading through the children's responses should help you to evaluate the success of your work on self-esteem with the children.

Section 2 Training workshops for mid-day supervisors (MDSs) and other adults

It is important that all adults are included in the raising self-esteem programme. There are six workshop sessions. You may like to invite other occasional adult workers to the first three workshops, while the second three are solely for MDSs. Those for MDSs will need to be funded in order to make sure that all attend. It is suggested that you hold these sessions either before the school meals staff start work or during the afternoon at the end of the school lunch hour when the  school meals staff have had their lunch. One senior member of staff should take the session with another observing and encouraging the school meals staff to participate.

Mid-day supervisors have for too long been left to find their own way of doing their work. Nowadays many primary schools initiate training sessions to help MDSs to identify ways to improve their work and to better understand the needs of children. Sessions such as these workshops enhance the status of MDSs, giving them confidence and raising their self-esteem, as well as providing a platform for training and for discussing concerns. If we embark on a whole school programme for enhancing self-esteem in the children everyone has to be involved. You could devise a certificate of attendance to bestow on participants after the course or use the one in the appendix and on the CD.

The mid-day team

The MDSs should feel that they are part of a team of people to ensure that children not only enjoy their school meal in civilised and safe surroundings, but that they also have a stimulating and enjoyable play session.

This team feeling can be fostered through regular meetings, some of which will be training sessions. Each school will decide how to fund the extra time that MDSs need to spend in school for these sessions. When the school is closed to children for teacher in-service training, MDSs are sometimes paid a retainer. Some schools ask them to come in for meetings or sessions in lieu of this.

The mid-day team will often consist of:

- the head or deputy head teacher responsible for organising training
- a teacher designated as lunchtime co-ordinator who will liaise between MDSs and teaching staff
- a senior MDS who will liaise between all MDSs and teachers. This person can be chosen informally or elected by the MDSs.

Before embarking on the workshop sessions for MDSs it is important to explain to them why the school is embarking on a self-esteem programme. It is hoped that this will lead to a significant improvement in the self-esteem in children which will, in turn have a positive impact on the children's learning. It is also important to stress that adults, too, may have low self-esteem and that through the programme it is hoped that all adults will recognise their strengths and benefit from increased self-esteem.

Overview

One of the first things for MDSs to realise is that children need to feel that MDSs care for them, that they are important to them and that they will listen to them and help them.

Qualities a good MDS will display are of:

- happiness when working with children
- patience
- the skill to be a good listener
- a sense of humour
- a positive outlook
- enjoyment of the responsibility
- an ability to keep control in an easy and positive way
- maintaining confidentiality; between adults and children both in and out of school.

Some schools have a play policy although in most cases this is not separate but embedded in general school policies. There should be a rationale for and a commitment for play provision together with a plan for putting the policy into action. MDSs may need training to understand and implement the school policy. Some schools employ staff as play supervisors and these could be invited to attend all the workshops. If you do not have a play policy yet, visit 'Ready Steady Play', a national play policy on the following website for ideas: http://www.omc.gov.ie/documents/publications/NCOPlay Policy_eng.pdf

There will be sanctions already in place in the school for children who behave badly. Make sure that the MDSs know what they are and how to implement them. They should take such a child to one side, speak carefully and quietly about the incident and make it easy for the child to be sorry and apologise. Meeting anger with sorrow does work; it calms the child down and helps them to regain control. Meeting anger with anger only inflames the situation as does arguing back; we need to give the child time to accept their lack of control and deal with it.

Training sessions

If you already have termly training sessions for MDSs, you could use the next one of these as your pre-training session. In this way you can inform MDSs of the value of the work the school is going to undertake, ask for their co-operation and set up regular meetings during one term to coincide with the teacher in-service programme. For the self-esteem programme to succeed it is essential that MDSs are involved and co-operate.

School handbook

When you have completed the self-esteem workshops, discuss with the MDSs the section in your school handbook that is about lunchtime play sessions and supervision of the mid-day meal.

Ask MDSs to think about how this section could be updated and what else they think should be included. Ask them all in turn to suggest changes or updates using a flip chart to record their responses. These responses could be taken to the next staff and governors' meetings and updates agreed.

Pre-training session

This is your opportunity to get to know the MDSs, to explain about the self-esteem programme and to let them know that they are valued members of the school. The training sessions should take place in a warm, friendly and comfortable atmosphere. It would be socially beneficial to start with a drink of tea or coffee, sit in comfortable chairs to help the MDSs to relax and get over any nerves.

Preparation

comfortable venue
relaxing
surroundings
welcome
provide each MDS
with a notebook.

After welcoming them and explaining about the self-esteem programme, discuss the best time and place for the workshop sessions and make sure that they all understand the importance of their full involvement.

After agreeing venues and times, ask the MDSs to spend some time to think about their own job description. Ask them to work in pairs or threes and to write down what they think their responsibilities and duties are. A general discussion about what the MDSs write will lead to agreement of what you as training organiser and they as the practitioners think their job should consist of.

You may like to build this up on a flip chart from their suggestions. This job description could then be agreed and copies made for them to put in their notebooks. It could also be inserted into the school handbook.

Explain that arrangements will be made for each of them to share a Circle Time session with the teacher and some or all of children they normally work with. They will need to liaise with the teachers concerned to set a time and date for this.

Circle Time session

MDSs need the support and recognition of the whole school, teachers, adults and children and one way to initiate this is to invite them to take part in a Circle Time session with the class they work with. This is most useful if it can take place at the start of the school year or term, or when a new MDS is appointed.

If the class is used to Circle Time this should prove to be an enjoyable and enlightening session for all. If the class is not used to Circle Time, the class teacher will need to set this up and have a few sessions before inviting the MDS to join them. There are many books about how to run a successful Circle Time.

Make sure that all the children are seated in a circle with older children on chairs or younger children on the floor. The teacher and MDS are seated at opposite sides of the circle with other classroom assistants spread evenly. Introduce or welcome the MDS by name and, starting with yourself introduce yourself ask all the children and your MDS in turn to finish this sentence, 'My name is...'

Ask the children to finish the sentence, 'I like lunchtimes because...' Allow children to 'pass'. Jot down their responses.

Ask everyone (self and MDS included) to finish the following sentences, jotting down their responses.

'I like eating my lunch (or dinner) because...'

'I don't like eating my lunch when...'

'I like lunchtimes when...'

'I don't like lunchtimes when...'

'I like lunchtime play outside because...'

'I don't like lunchtime play outside when...'

'I like wet day lunchtime play because...'

'I don't like wet day lunchtime play when...'

> **Outdoor lunch play is good because...**
>
> it's fun to run about
> we can play games
> we play with our friends
> we sit and talk
> the MDS is kind to us
> there are games to play
> we can play with children from other classes
> we can run off steam
> we learn new games
> we know the rules
> we can tell jokes
> we can be quiet
> it's fun in the playground
> we take turns on the climbing frame.

You may choose to spread this work over several Circle Time sessions for younger children, perhaps during the time immediately before the lunch break starts so that the MDS can easily plan to be there. Alternatively, you may ask, say, six children only to finish each sentence before going on to the next. You might prefer to ask young children to work in pairs to decide how to finish their sentence.

At the end of the Circle Time discuss with the MDS what has been revealed by the children. In some cases you may wish to take action to remedy any concerns. You may want to use the children's responses to make a class display.

Workshop 1　Let's be positive

Time　Min: 35 minutes　Max: 50 minutes

Focus on

- celebrating the strengths, skills and experiences which mid-day supervisors bring with them to their workplace
- remembering to use positive words when talking to children.

Materials

flipchart
paper
pens
copies of negative remarks list
MDSs will need their notebooks.

Organisation

Make sure that there are sufficient chairs arranged in a circle.

Allow a few minutes for the group to settle and welcome the participants.

Activity 1: 10–15 mins

Sitting in a circle, ask the MDSs to think of all the things they have done this morning before they came to school. Ask them to think of all the hats they could have worn, for example, a chef's cap for making the breakfast. Ask them all to tell you two hats they could have worn this morning. List these on the flip chart.

This list will demonstrate to MDSs the multiple skills that they share and bring to your school. Give them a metaphorical pat on the back as you celebrate all these skills.

Negative remarks

You're shouting again Jane.
Stop making that silly noise.
We're not going in until you stop all this talking.
Your hands are dirty.
Stop pushing in the dinner line.
You're too noisy.
Telling tales again are we?
Stop quarrelling you two.
I'm tired of telling you, don't do that.
Oh, not you again, what's up now?

Activity 2: 15–20 mins

Give a copy of the Negative Remarks list to each pair of MDSs. Ask each pair to read through the list and turn these negative remarks into positive ones. Give five minutes for them to write down their new list.

Ask them to exchange their list with someone else several times and then in turn to read out to the whole group the revised first sentence on the paper they are holding. Ask them to choose the best revised version, or amalgamate some and write this up on the flipchart.

Do this with each of the positive remarks in turn.

Discussion: 10–15 mins

Talk about the importance of making children feel good about themselves, of forgiving lapses and helping children to behave better.

Ask the MDSs to focus on being positive with the children. Ask them, over the next few days, to jot down in their notebooks any examples of when they feel that they have been able to do this well. Explain that you will want to share these at the next workshop.

Workshop 2   Use of voice: getting attention

Time   Min: 30 minutes   Max: 45 minutes

Focus on

- words to use and not use with children
- tone of voice
- privacy and consideration
- remembering to use positive words when talking to children.

Materials

flipchart
paper
pens.

Organisation

Make sure that there are sufficient chairs arranged in a circle.

Opening Activity: 5–10 mins

Allow a few minutes for the group to settle.

Ask for examples of good practice that they will have noted in their notebooks. Discuss these.

Activity 1: 10–15 mins

Explain to the MDSs that it is important to make best use of their voice.

Ask them to work in pairs to talk about:

- ▶ not raising their voice or shouting at children
- ▶ not using sarcasm
- ▶ not arguing with children
- ▶ not being rude back.

Ask each pair to write down on slips of paper some advice about how to best use their voice when dealing with children in the dinner hall, the playground, the classroom.

Collect the slips of paper and read out to the group what they have suggested. Do some need revising? Can they all agree on a useful reminder list?

Tip

Explain that if they make a remark to a child in a group, the child won't know who they are talking to, unless they use the child's name. It is no good saying their name at the end, because s/he will have missed what has been said. The best way to get a child's attention is always to use the name first, for example: 'Jane, you did that very well.'

Reminder list

keep voice...
low
steady
warm
kind
encouraging
responsive
caring

Activity 2: 10–15 mins

Ask volunteers to say how they gain the attention of children in the classroom. List these on the flipchart. Discuss whether these are really good ideas or whether they can invent a better way.

Final moments: 5 mins

Before the end of the session, make sure that there is time for discussion and that everyone feels good about contributing to it. Is their own self-esteem increasing?

Remind the MDSs to use their notebooks to record all useful hints gained during the session.

> **Attention signals**
>
> raise a hand until all do this
>
> chant 'Are you ready?' – children respond with 'Yes we are.'
>
> clap a pattern, children repeat

Workshop 3   Maintaining good behaviour

Time   Min: 40 minutes   Max: 55 minutes

Focus on

- understanding their role in helping children to maintain good
- behaviour
- rules
- reprimands
- incentives.

Materials

flipchart, paper, pens, one copy for each person of the school's play policy behaviour policy playground rules.

Activity 1: Positive behaviour 15–20 mins

Welcome the MDSs to the group and explain that this session is to be about maintaining good behaviour. Ask them to work in pairs and to write down on slips of paper the kinds of behaviour that they want in the playground, classroom or dinner hall. Remind them to keep these positive – a list of 'dos' rather than a list of 'don'ts'.

Ask a spokesperson from each pair to read out their list and ask someone to write these down on the flipchart, ticking the original where there is repetition.

Talk about the behaviour they are expecting from the children – is it realistic?

Ask them all, as a group, to use the ideas on the flipchart to make one useful list of the kind of behaviour you want from the children – a list that could be displayed in the classroom, so that the children know what the MDSs expect of them.

Play policy

If you have a play policy make sure that the MDSs each have a copy of this to keep in their notebook.

Positive behaviour

being kind and caring to one another
playing co-operatively
sharing equipment
listening to each other
joining in games
letting other children join in
being truthful
having fun in a sensible way
making sure they don't hurt people's feelings
making sure their games aren't upsetting others
being considerate
showing respect to each other
respect for property
willing to help
showing good manners
being polite
waiting turns
playing fairly.

Activity 2: Playground rules 10–15 mins

Talk about your playground situation. Are there places where:

- ▶ children could be hidden from view
- ▶ children should not go
- ▶ they would not be safe
- ▶ they could be led into mischief?

Ask the MDSs to help you to list these kinds of places in your school on the flipchart. How can we prevent children from going to these places? What rules would they like?

Working in pairs, ask the MDSs to draw up a list of playground rules that they would like to put in place. Come together as a group and discuss these one by one.

Read out your school's playground rules. Do the two lists match? Could you add to your playground rules from what the MDSs say?

Activity 3: Reprimands 5 mins
Talk about the importance of adhering to the school sanctions when children behave badly. Can they:

- ▶ take children on one side to do this
- ▶ make sure that the child knows that it is the poor behaviour they don't like, not the child
- ▶ make it easy for children to regain control, apologise to you and others
- ▶ forgive and help them to re-join their friends?

Have you a behaviour policy for your school? if so, does the MDS's list match this policy? Read out, or give copies of the behaviour policy to the MDSs. They could keep a copy in their notebooks.

Activity 4: Incentives 10–15 mins
Explain that maintaining good behaviour is all about over-praising good behaviour while ignoring (where it is safe to do so) poor or unco-operative behaviour. Talk with the group about the kinds of incentives that will help children to want to behave well, both in the dinner hall and playground.

Ask them for their suggestions about ways to reward good behaviour and jot these down on the flip chart. Are these practical? Can they be implemented? This will depend, to some extent, on the way teachers in class and other adults in school reward good behaviour. Some schools have a 'golden book' where good behaviour is recorded; lunchtime behaviour could be included here.

Have they thought about:

- ▶ lunchtime helper badges
- ▶ playground helper badges
- ▶ stickers?

Discuss how they would organise and use these rewards and incentives. Remind the MDSs that we are seeking to help to raise children's self-esteem and that some children will need more help than others.

> **Lunchtime stickers for:**
>
> careful eating
> helpful in dinner hall
> eating well
> helpful in playground
> smiley face for improvement
> playground helper
> play equipment helper
> good manners
> fair play.

Final moments

Allow time for MDSs to voice any concerns or put forward any ideas they have before winding up the session.

Workshop 4   In the dinner hall/classroom

Time   Min: 35 minutes   Max: 55 minutes

Materials

flipchart paper
pens.

Focus on

- understanding the need for dinner time routine
- how to make this a happy time for everyone.

Activity 1: Worries 10–15 mins

Explain to the MDSs that you want to get their views on the dinner hall and ask them to think for a few minutes about the present situation at your school.

Ask them to work in pairs and jot down three good things about the dinner hall arrangements. Come together as a group and talk about all these good things.

Ask them to work in different pairs and to write down three things that are difficult in the dinner hall – things that cause them to feel less than happy or that worry them.

Come together as a group and talk about these worrying things. Discuss ways that these worries can be addressed and whether changes in organisation could help.

Activity 2: Rewards and sanctions 10–15 mins

It is important to maintain positive behaviour in the dinner hall where children may be moving about with plates of food.

Ask the MDS to work in pairs and jot down some answers to the following:

How can they:

- ▶ make sure that children move carefully and with consideration in the dinner hall
- ▶ gain children's attention
- ▶ reward children for good and helpful behaviour?

Dinner hall rewards

say 'well done'
give a smile
touch shoulder
show you appreciate them
praise the child
pass on praise to class teacher
allow them to help
badges or stickers.

Come together in the group and discuss their ideas. Will they work? Which are best? Make a list of the best ideas.

Ask them to write the list of good ideas in their notebooks.

Activity 3: Manners and eating habits 5–10 mins

Talk about the importance of being a role model to the children. Ask the group to consider what they can do to be a good role model in the dinner hall and write up their suggestions on the flipchart.

Ask them to make a list of how they would like children to behave in the dinner hall.

Children need to know that they matter, that they are important to us.

> **In the dinner hall, we want children to:**
>
> wait their turn
> talk quietly to each other
> listen to the music
> keep their chairs quiet
> walk carefully
> keep to the rules.

Ask the group to discuss in pairs what they can do to show the children that they are important and that they matter. Come together and share their ideas.

Activity 4: Where and when you sit 10–15 mins

Ask the MDS to think of a recent occasion when they went out to eat in a restaurant. Ask them to try to identify what made it a memorable occasion and why they enjoyed it. Jot down any interesting suggestions on the flipchart. Talk about these.

Discuss how they would have felt if:

- ▶ they had to sit with people they didn't know
- ▶ there were friends nearby, having fun and they couldn't join in because the table was full
- ▶ they had to eat very early or very late because of the restaurant's opening hours
- ▶ they were given food they didn't like and were made to eat it all up
- ▶ they were not allowed to have a drink whenever they liked
- ▶ they always missed the best meals because they always had to be last in.

Ask if they think the writing on the flipchart and the above discussion could refer to school meals? Ask the group to try to think of the dinner hall as a restaurant for the children and the school meal as the children's restaurant dinner.

Final moments

Ask the MDSs, this week, to concentrate on noticing examples of how children are feeling when they are in the dinner hall and to write these down in their notebooks. These will form the basis for discussion at the start of the next session.

Workshop 5   In the playground

Time   Min: 40 minutes   Max: 60 minutes

Focus on

- safety in the playground, good quality play playleaders
- ways to make this a happy time for everyone.

Review from the last session

Ask the MDSs to read out their examples of how they think that children felt in the dinner hall. Discuss whether these are good or not so good feelings and what we can all do about them.

Activity 1: Health and safety in the playground 10–15 mins

Discuss your playground situation – the various surfaces, tarmac, grass, play surfaces. Talk about any permanent apparatus and how you allocate children to play on it. What are the rules and do they work?

Ask the MDSs to work in pairs and to jot down any concerns they have about the way playground play is organised. Address these concerns as a group.

Talk about the routine for children who fall or are hurt in the playground. Ask them, in pairs to write down the steps that are necessary when someone falls and hurts their head.

First Aid

assess the damage
take to medical room
find first aider
using gloves, treat wound
make note in accident book
seek professional help if necessary
reassure child
inform teacher.

Activity 2: Organisation of play leaders 10–15 mins

Ask the group to think of various ways of organising play through buddies or play leaders from older children. Jot down their ideas on the flipchart. Can they agree on one way that will work in your school?

Perhaps they will have:

- ▶ two play leaders to each class, responsible to the MDSs who will suggest today's game
- ▶ several play leaders in their own area of the playground each with their own game to offer to children from any classes
- ▶ one designated area for ball games, one for ring games, one for wall games, etc.

Activity 3: Training play leaders 10–15 mins

The lunchtime break can be a very long time for children who do not have good play skills. Using older children as play leaders can free MDSs to keep an eye on all the children and not be concerned with a small group.

Ask the group to think about how these play leaders could be trained and jot down their ideas on the flipchart.

> **Play leaders could:**
>
> wear a badge
> wear a band
> take complete control of the game
> organise the equipment
> collect and return the equipment
> choose who will play.

Have they thought about:

- ▶ how to choose which children shall be leaders
- ▶ organising and allocating equipment
- ▶ where games can be safely played
- ▶ how to ring the changes of children playing each game
- ▶ use of permanent play apparatus
- ▶ recognising and enhancing status of play leaders.

Examine the box of play apparatus. Is it comprehensive enough? What else could be added to make it more useful? Discuss how to make sure that it is all collected and returned at the end of the lunch session.

Activity 4: Monitoring the effectiveness of play leaders 10–15 mins

Play leaders are only as good as the training they receive. If they are trained buddies they will already have skills that will help them with younger children. If not, what skills do the MDSs think the play leaders should have?

> **Play leaders are...**
>
> responsible
> fun
> fair
> organised
> flexible
> in control
> kind
> open to all children.

Ask them to discuss this in pairs and jot down their ideas.

Come together as a group and share all these ideas. Will they all work? Will they all be practical?

Ask the group to consider how they will handle:

- ▶ play leaders who become officious or bossy
- ▶ children who do not play fairly
- ▶ children who spoil the game
- ▶ children who are waiting to join in or see their exclusion as unfair
- ▶ games that get out of hand, disrupt or spoil other children's play
- ▶ arguments between play leaders and other play leaders or other children.

After this discussion tell the participants that the next workshop will be about wet day provision and ask them to jot down any concerns they have to bring to the next session.

Workshop 6   Wet days

Time   Min: 50 minutes   Max: 60 minutes

Focus on

- the organisation, routine of wet days, indoor play
- ways to make this a happy time for all.

> **Materials**
>
> flipchart
> paper
> pens
> certificates of attendance
> (see CD and appendix for
> example).

Activity 1: Who's in charge? 10–15 mins

It can be difficult for MDSs to know what they can allow children to do and what they must not allow them to do in the classroom on wet days. Children may say one thing and teachers another. It is essential to get the ground rules right.

Ask the group to work in pairs and to make a list of the things that they would like to have available for the children to play with or do during wet dinner playtimes.

Share these lists and discuss whether all these ideas are possible. Ask the MDSs to show their list to the class teacher later, discuss what is possible and write these up somewhere in the classroom for the children to see.

Activity 2: Communication 10–15 mins

There may be more time to interact with children on wet days in the classroom. Ask the group to consider ways to interact well with individual children.

How can they do this?

Jot down what they say on the flipchart.

Have they included things in this list?

Ask them to make a complete list to write down in their notebooks.

> **Communication**
>
> Listen carefully to what they say.
> Be interested and show it.
> Look at their face.
> Engage eye contact.
> Make encouraging sounds to help them to continue.
> Don't let others interrupt.
> Ask them to think of, and tell you, their own solutions to problems or disagreements.
> Make them feel good about themselves.

Activity 3: Clearing and tidying up 10–15 mins

Ask the group to think about the end of indoor play sessions and their responsibility to get the classroom back to normal before the teacher comes back. What kinds of things can they do or say to children to help with this tidying up?

Use the flipchart for their responses.

Remind them that the children are used to clearing up their own mess, but that they will need encouragement; the youngest children may need plenty of time to do this well.

Activity 4: Playing quiet games with children 10–15 mins

It is often useful at the end of an indoor play session to tidy up and then read a story to the children, or play sit down games such as 'Simon says'.

Ask the group to share the games that they think are good for children to play at this time.

Make a list on the flipchart.

Ask them to explain how to play any games that people do not know.

Ask them to collect as many of these games as possible and write them down to share with others. Perhaps the children can help to add to the list.

You could then duplicate these so that all MDSs can have a copy.

Activity 5: Telling stories and poems to children 10–15 mins

Ask the group to tell you how they choose story/poetry books to read to children on wet days and jot down what they say.

Explain that reading stories is much easier when they have already read the story and know what is coming. Do they sometimes 'edit' stories as they are reading? Do they explain difficult words? Do they talk about the story after they have read to the children?

Have they thought of visiting the library and reading new children's books for themselves? Can they tell, not read, the stories they know and love?

> **Do they:**
>
> use the class library
> the school library
> use the public library
> tell stories that they know
> tell stories about their childhood
> let the children choose
> read children's own books
> sing rhymes with the children
> ask 'good readers' to read a story?

Final discussion

Remind the participants that, last time they were asked to bring to this discussion any concerns they had about wet day provision. Ask if all these concerns have now been addressed and discuss any that have not.

You may like to give each of the participants a list of the 'Do's and don'ts' on the following page.

Thank them all for their participation, congratulate them for attending and ensure that they realise how very much they are valued as members of the school. If you are awarding certificates of attendance do it now.

Do's and Don'ts for MDSs

Use an assertive approach

DO

- treat all children fairly and equally
- adopt a friendly and approachable manner
- use polite respectful language
- be calm, confident, positive and purposeful
- take an interest in each child
- build positive relationships with children
- scan carefully and intervene early
- give clear, positively worded instructions
- have rules that are well understood by all
- use low key cues and rule reminders
- have clear routines and systems in place
- catch children behaving well; tell them that you are pleased
- give children time to follow instructions
- maintain confidentiality about children and adults in and out of school.

Avoid being aggressive

DON'T

- lose your cool
- appear tense, angry and aggressive
- jump in without knowing the full story
- invade children's personal space or use threatening gestures
- argue, shout or use personal insults
- be sarcastic
- label children.

Avoid being ineffectual

DON'T

- convey uncertainty and lack of confidence
- avoid eye contact
- be vague
- use a pleading tone
- give up.

Resources

Guidelines for Midday Supervisory Assistants. WEST, c/o Library & Heritage HQ, Bythesea Road, Trowbridge, Wiltshire, BA148BS.

Making a Meal of It, J. Matthews and R. Hurn, Pearson Publishing, Cambridge email info@pearson.co.uk, www.pearsonpublishing.co.uk

Search the web – 'outdoor games' gives lots of ideas www.amazon.com
Search under 'books', then 'playground games' for book ideas, e.g. *The Ultimate Playground and Recess Game Book* by Guy Bailey.

Section 3 Training workshops for teachers and classroom assistants

Introduction

Each of these sessions should be of no longer than an hour, excluding time for discussion and reflection. Ideally, all sessions should take place as a regular part of in-service training in one term of the school year. Weekly sessions would be beneficial. It is suggested that the sessions take place after school although some schools may need to use part of the lunch time break.

Busy teachers may need to be convinced of the need to spend time in enhancing children's self-esteem. In fact, some teachers may feel that certain children have all too much self-esteem! You may need to explain that it is easier for children who have positive self-esteem to resist persuasion, peer pressure and bullying. This will become more important as primary school children grow into adolescence and have to face temptations such as early sexual activity, smoking, alcohol and drug abuse. Those with positive self-esteem are more able to talk to people about these issues; they are better informed, can accept advice and thus able to make up their own mind about how to act.

A child who has high self-esteem is able to stand up and say 'no'.

Use these sessions as part of your PSHE training and hopefully both under and over confident children will learn about themselves, how to treat others and how they themselves like to be treated. The lessons and activities should help those children with low self-esteem to become more confident and more able to take a more positive role in their own learning.

There are seven training sessions for teachers and other adults who work in classrooms alongside the children.

Session 1 is a discussion of the Draw and Write children's base line response sheets.

Session 2 is an overview of self-esteem and suggests that the first short topic, 'Being positive' is completed with the children before the next session

Session 3 to 6 each first review the completed topic, contain other activities before identifying a new short topic to be completed before the next session.

Session 7 will follow up the topic from session 6 and consider the responses of a repeat of the Draw and Write research strategy. It will be a discussion and evaluation of how far the children and adults in your school have moved towards higher self-esteem.

Session 1   the 'Am I confident?' responses

Time   Min: 30 minutes.   Max: 60 minutes
(this will depend on the size of school)

Focus on

- good self-esteem
- positive responses from the children.

It is suggested that teachers implement the
Draw and Write research strategy a week before
the first session. This will allow time for teachers
to read through the children's responses. If all
teachers use the data collection sheet to collect
numerical data, the figures through each year group can be collated to produce a good
picture of how children in each year group feel. You may like to gather all the data
together to provide teachers with overall school figures of the children's responses. As
children's responses are anonymous, resist temptation to identify children by their
drawings or writing.

While it is relatively easy for one form entry schools to discuss the findings from the
Draw and Write, it may be more useful for large primary schools to organise these
sessions for separate infant or junior teachers or even in single or double year groups.

Boxes 1 and 2

Discuss how many of the children have drawn themselves with a happy face in Box 1.
Most young children will draw a smile; therefore the number of children who have not
done so could be significant.

Discuss how many of the children have written about supportive teachers and friends.
Are there more friends mentioned than teachers or other adults? Does this tell us
something about our adult support for children?

How many children have mentioned being stimulated by interesting and appropriate
work? Do you think that these figures reflect the kind of teaching throughout the school?

How many children mention play in some form or other? Young children may mention
the play house or games and activities at use in the classroom; older children may
mention sports or games. What children have, and have not, mentioned may be
significant and may cause you to re-think the play options of children at your school.

What do the children in your school think about your resources? What have they specifically mentioned or not mentioned? Could you be providing resources that are overlooked by children?

Boxes 3 and 4
Again look at the expression on the face of the children in the drawings. Are some of these 'not happy' children still smiling?

What kinds of feelings do the children write about? Collect a list of these if you can; if there are too many, identify any that cause concern and discuss what you can do about this.

Look carefully at the people that the children say could help them. Who are these people in your school? Are they the children's own friends or family members? Are they specific class teachers or are they other adults in the school that the children feel confident about asking for help? How can you extend support for children?

What kind of worries do the children mention in their responses? Are they school specific and can you do something about them at school? Are they child specific that may cause you to re-think school behaviour or play policies?

Boxes 5, 6, 7, 8
The responses in these boxes will tell you a lot about how confident the children feel in your school buildings and surroundings. Have they identified any places where they feel are unsafe or uncomfortable? Discuss what you can do about this.

Have they mentioned specific teachers or other adults whom they feel safe with and are able to talk about problems or are the people who can help them always other children and friends? What can you do about this?

Have any of the children mentioned bullying or negative feelings such as fear of places or people? Discuss what you can do about this.

Discuss whether the Draw and Write activity has given a happy and healthy picture of your school. Does the Draw and Write show the children as confident and with good self-esteem? If not, discuss how this can be remedied.

Session 2 Why promote self-esteem?

Preparation

Either duplicate the following 5 visuals on flip chart,
provide OHP visuals or
use the visuals from the CD on PowerPoint.

Promoting Children's Mental Health Within Early Years and School Settings, Dfee 2001

'Mental health is about maintaining a good level of personal and social functioning.

For children and young people, this means getting on with others both peers and adults participating in educative and other social activities and having a positive self-esteem.'

As adults we tend to do the things we are
good at and avoid the things we are bad at.

In schools we find the things that children
can't do, e.g. read – and make them do
more if it!

No sooner have they reached a target than
we push them on to the next.

Session 2 visual 2 Self-Concept = self-image, ideal self, self-esteem

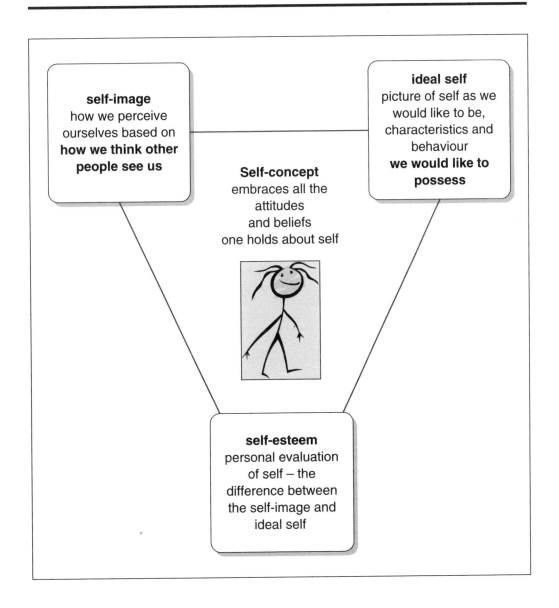

self-image
how we perceive
ourselves based on
**how we think other
people see us**

ideal self
picture of self as we
would like to be,
characteristics and
behaviour
**we would like to
possess**

Self-concept
embraces all the
attitudes
and beliefs
one holds about self

self-esteem
personal evaluation
of self – the
difference between
the self-image and
ideal self

Session 2 visual 3   A child with high self-esteem views himself as a success

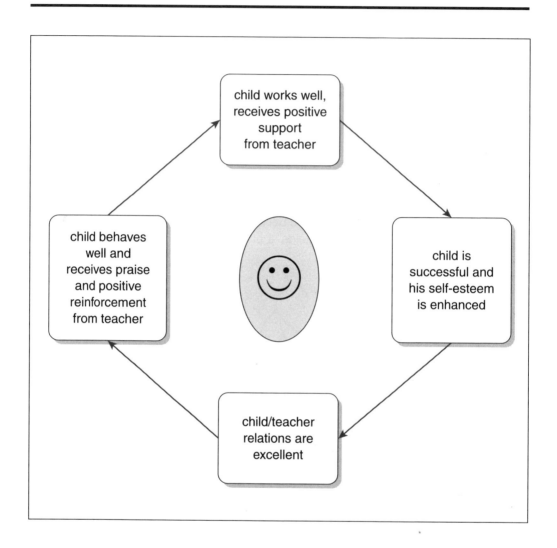

Session 2 visual 4   A child with low self-esteem views himself a failure

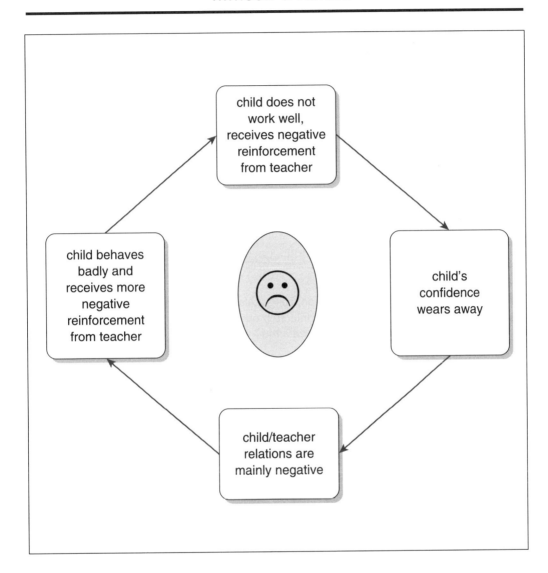

Session 2 Why promote self-esteem?

Time Min: 40 minutes   Max: 60 minutes

Focus on

- self-concept
- poor self-esteem
- good self-esteem.

Activity 1: Why promote self-esteem 3–5 mins

Show visual 1, why we need to promote self-esteem.

Allow three to five minutes for discussion, concentrating on:

- ▶ do we pressure children to perform?
- ▶ do we give enough time for reflection, congratulation and celebration?
- ▶ are we guilty of praising what the children produce in terms of work rather than in terms of personal development and improved attitude?

Activity 2: Self-concept 10–15 mins

Show visual 2, self-concept

Allow time for comments from the floor before concentrating on the following.

How is our self-concept formed? If it is based on how other people perceive us, how can we, as teachers, improve children's self-concept? It won't be through dwelling on children's failures, or through being harsh or unkind about poor work. Can we show all children that we perceive them in a positive light, even if their work may be of a low standard? Can we concentrate on the positive, the good points and ignore the negative?

Can we, through interaction with children help them to concentrate on what they would like themselves to be? Can we get them to focus on their ideal self? Are we big enough to be able to show our own ideal self to the children and indicate how we are striving to improve?

Can we look at self-esteem as a combination of what other people think of us and what we are striving to be? Older primary children will be able to grasp this idea. Younger primary children will need it putting into context and here children's stories can help, for example, Cinderella's sisters perceived her as dull, useless and a drudge. It took the fairy godmother to lift Cinderella out of that self-concept and give her the self-esteem to go to the ball.

Activity 3: Using literature 10–15 mins

Ask teachers to work in pairs and to discuss which other books and stories could be used to illustrate that self-concept and self-esteem are linked; these can be used with children. Ask them to jot down any titles they think are suitable. Ask them to read out their suggested titles and discuss how these could be used. Ask the teachers to find one more book that would be really useful, to use it and to bring it to the next session to discuss how they used it.

Activity 4: High self-esteem 8–10 mins

Show visual 3 and allow time for discussion. Ask volunteers to tell you of any examples of how they have massaged a child's self-esteem with good results. If using PowerPoint show the seven pictures that children have drawn about feeling good.

Activity 5: Low self-esteem 8–10 mins

Show visual 4 and allow time for discussion. Ask for examples of how this kind of thing may have happened in classrooms or in other areas around the school.

Final activity: 3–5 minutes

Ask teachers to examine their practice with children in their class and think of ways they have promoted self-esteem in the past.

Ask them to select one child with poor self-esteem and during the coming week to seek ways to improve this child's self-esteem. Ask them to jot down one example of how they tried to do this and to bring to the next session.

Work with the children

Use the lessons and activity sheets for 'Being positive' with the children before the next session.

Session 3   What can we do?

Time   Min: 45 minutes   Max: 60 minutes

Focus on

- using children's names
- emphasising the positive
- looking for things to praise
- same different and special.

Being positive: 5 mins

Discuss this work you did with the children. Were there any relevant findings? Have any children shown any increase in self-esteem yet?

Books: 5 mins

Ask each teacher to show the book they used since the last session and to say how they used it to improve self-esteem. Make a list of the useful books and ask teachers to try to add to this list.

Activity 1: Examples of raising one child's self-esteem 10 mins

Remind the group that they all had a task to do for this session; this was to find a child with low self-esteem and to consciously try to raise it.

Ask volunteers to contribute to a discussion about what they have been able to do.

Discuss whether this was successful and whether another ploy would have been better.

Discuss whether these interventions to improve a child's self-esteem are likely to have long lasting results.

Preparation

Obtain a copy of the picture book *Nothing* by Mike Inkpen.

Use visual 5 on PowerPoint, duplicate these ten sentences or write them on the flip chart.

- You're wasting time again Jane.
- Don't keep tapping your pencil like that.
- Don't make that noise James.
- We won't go out until you show me you are ready.
- Stop shouting Imram.
- This work is not good enough.
- No you can't.
- Stop pushing in the line.
- This is the noisiest class in the school.
- Your writing is disgraceful.

Use visual 6 or write these on the flip chart.

- Help children to know that they matter.
- Look for and find things to praise.
- Give lots of praise.
- Ignore or make light of things that they do wrong.
- Use their names first.
- Find useful tasks for them to do.
- Give them responsibility.
- Say 'I know you can do it.

Activity 2: How to recognise low self-esteem 10–15 mins

Ask the group to think of a child in their class who has really low self-esteem and, without naming the child, to work in pairs to write how this low self-esteem shows itself. After five minutes ask each group to double up with another and share their ideas, crossing off those that are superfluous, making one list.

Ask a volunteer from each four to read out their list and make one list on the flipchart or OHP.

Discuss these ways of recognising low self-esteem. Ask each person in the group to reflect on behaviour of other children in their class, based on the list they made, which might lead them to think they could have low self-esteem. Ask them to make a private list of these children and think of ways to help them.

Activity 3: Talking to children 10–15 mins

Discuss the advantages of using children's names first when talking to them. Hearing one's names helps children to tune in immediately and grab their attention.

Discuss the advantage of using only positive language with children; the do's rather than the don'ts. Using negative remarks focuses the child's mind on the negative and could encourage them to comply with the negative message. For example, if you say 'Don't tip your chair back like that,' someone will always do it just to see what happens.

Use visual 5 or your list on the flipchart and show the group the ten negative remarks and say you want them to turn the sentences into positive ones. Ask the group to work in pairs and ask half of them to start with sentence one and the rest to start with sentence ten and work backwards.

After about ten minutes, stop the participants and ask each pair to read one sentence in its positive form. Have they all said a child's name first? Ask them to focus on this positivity during the next week and to report back at the next session.

Read through **visual 6** or the flipchart and discuss how they can integrate this positivity into their teaching.

Activity 4: *Nothing* 10 mins

Read the story of *Nothing* to the whole group. Talk about the self-esteem of the toy and how this increases as he is recognised, accepted, re-discovered and loved.

Ask the group to think of using this book with children. They could talk with the children about the feelings that this toy would have had and think about his feelings when:

- ▶ he had no name
- ▶ someone said he was nothing
- ▶ when characters seemed to recognise him
- ▶ as he began to remember things about himself
- ▶ when he was 'found' by his family.

Ask them how would they feel if someone said they were nothing.

For next session

If it is not already there, ask teachers to add *Nothing* to their list of self-esteem stories and to read it to their class noting any interesting observations that the children make.

Work with the children

Use the lesson and activity sheet 'Same, different and special' with the children before the next session.

Nothing by Mike Inkpen, 1995. London, Hodder Children's Books.

Session 4 Valuing ourselves

Time Min: 42 minutes Max: 63 minutes

Focus on

- valuing ourselves
- helping children to value themselves
- re-enforcing praise.

Introductory activity: 5 mins

Ask the participants to tell the group of any interesting observations that the children make after listening to *Nothing*. How did they as teachers feel when the children were trying to explain their feelings?

Same, different and special: 5–10 mins

Discuss the lesson and activity sheets on 'Same, different and special' that you have done with the children.

Activity 1: our skills 10–15 mins

Ask each participant to focus on their own skills. Ask them to finish the sentence:

'One thing I am really good at is…'

Jot down these skills on the flipchart.

When everyone has responded, look through the list of skills that your school possesses and praise all the participants for them.

> **Preparation**
>
> Duplicate these sentences, put them on OHP film or flipchart.
>
> - Jan does some good drawing.
> - Sam lends Mary a crayon.
> - Kieran gets the books ready for his table.
> - Zac lets Jake into the assembly line in front of him.
> - Aaron helps Sasha to find her book.
> - Jim holds the door open for you.
>
> Use visual 7 or jot it down and read it out.
>
> - Jan, I like the way you've done that, you've really tried hard with it.
> - Sam, that's really good the way you've helped Mary this morning.
> - Kieren, thanks for getting the books ready for your table.
> - Zac, thanks for letting Jake into the line, that was kind.
> - Aaron, it was kind of you to help Sasha to find her book.

Ask them to think about how they felt when they were telling the group about the thing that they are good at. What were these feelings and where did they feel them? How did they feel when you praised them for their skills? Remind them that children will feel just like this – and more – when their skills are recognised and when they are praised.

Activity 2: Positive and constructive praise 10–15 mins

Ask participants to tell you how they feel when someone praises them. Jot down the words they use. Remind them that many children, especially the young ones will not have this vocabulary to express their feelings but we can still give them the feelings if we use praise in a positive way.

Positive and constructive praise not only helps children to feel good about themselves it also helps children to remember your standards and expectations. It is a way of advertising what you find good about children's work and behaviour. It is a lost opportunity to just say 'good' or 'well done', put a tick or a smiley face on work.

Ask the participants to look through the sentences you have prepared and to write down what they would say to each child using re-enforcing praise. Have they used phrases such as the ones on **visual 7** or from the list you made?

Activity 3: Helping children to value themselves 10–15 mins

Ask the participants to work with a partner and jot down what they can do to help children to value themselves.

Allow 5 mins. Ask each group to work with another pair and make one list.

Allow 2 mins. Ask one from each four to read out their list. Jot these on the flip-chart, deleting any duplicates. Read through the list adding any more that participants think of.

> Help children to value themselves by asking them to:
> - think about what they are good at
> - give themselves praise for it
> - be proud of their own skills and achievements
> - talk to others they trust about how they are feeling
> - talk about things which they might find difficult
> - be good to themselves and treat themselves as special.

Work with the children

Use the topic and activity sheets on 'Feeling good' with the children before the next session.

Final activity: 2–3 mins

Explain that you want them to start thinking about using re-enforcing and constructive praise frequently with the children. Ask them to concentrate on this during the week and to jot down any good examples of what they said and the effect it had on the child and the rest of the class. You will want everyone to give one example to the group at the next session.

Session 5   Communication

Time   Min: 45 minutes   Max: 60 minutes

Focus on

- communication skills
- good behaviour

Opening activity: 10 mins

Remind the participants of their task you gave them last time and ask them to tell the group:

- ▶ one example of using re-enforcing and constructive praise
- ▶ the effect it had on that child
- ▶ the effect, if any, it had on the rest of the class
- ▶ the effect, if any, it had on you the teacher.

Discuss these examples.

Feeling good: 5–10 mins

Discuss the lesson and activity sheets on 'Feeling good' that you have done with the children.

Activity 2: Communication 10–15 mins

Ask the group to think about how to use communication in their aim to raise self-esteem in children.

Ask volunteers to say what tips they would give to new teachers when communicating with children to help to raise their self-esteem. List these on flip chart or OHP. Discuss each contribution and ask participants to put the list in order of usefulness.

Suggestions may include:

- listen carefully to what children say
- be interested and show it
- look at the child's face
- engage eye contact
- make encouraging sounds to help them to continue
- don't let others interrupt
- ask them to think of, and tell you, their own solutions to problems or disagreements.

Activity 3: Link good behaviour to child 10–15 mins

Linking good behaviour to children with poor self-esteem will help to raise it. Ask the group to think about a child they know who often behaves badly. This child, if regularly corrected will have low self-esteem.

Ask each participant to identify one child who has poor or unacceptable behaviour, to jot this down and work out a strategy for linking good behaviour to the child.

Come together as a group and discuss these strategies. Will they all work? Are some better than others?

> **One example**
>
> You could identify a child who is continually talking in class. Talk privately to the child about this behaviour and ask co-operation in changing it a step at a time. Say that in this one lesson, you will check on him every 3 minutes and if he is working well and not talking you will give a smiley face sticker. How many stickers can he collect in 30 minutes? Use a timer to check. Lengthen time in future lessons.

Closing activity: 5–10 mins

Read through the three sentences on **visual 8** or the flipchart and discuss.

Use **visual 9** and discuss.

Talk about Circle Time and how it can be used as a venue for PSHE and especially self-esteem. Ask the participants to use the following Circle Time activity before the next session to promote self-esteem in children.

Ask children to finish the sentence: 'I am… (name) and I am good at…'

List their responses on the board and after the children have all had a chance to respond talk about the list. Praise them for their abilities. Have you found out more about your children? Can you use some of these abilities in your classroom activities?

Write about one child with low self-esteem who has responded well to this and what you can to do enhance his self-esteem further.

Work with the children

Use the topic and activity sheets on 'Communication' with the children before the next session.

Session 6   Praise and rewards

Time   Min: 42 minutes   Max: 63 minutes

Focus on

- giving praise
- appropriate rewards.

Preparation

flipchart or
OHP pens

Opening activity: 10 mins

Ask participants to say how they fared with the Circle Time activity they were to do before this session. Compare successes. Ask participants to suggest other Circle Time activities that would raise children's self-esteem.

Activity 1: Communication 5–10 mins

Discuss the topic and activity sheets on 'Communication' that you have done with the children. Refer to their responses in the next two activities.

Activity 2: Praise 10–15 mins

Remind participants of how they feel when they are praised. Do you as adults praise each other? Could you do more?

Think about the kind of praises that we can give to children. Ask the group to work in pairs and jot down a list of the kinds of praise they use with the children in their classes. After 4 minutes ask them to join another pair and compare notes to make one list. After another 2 minutes come together as a group and list your methods of praise on the flip-chart or OHP.

Have they included smiling, verbal praise, tone of voice and touch as praise? What about catching them being good, thumbs up and showing them trust? Sometimes a smile at the right time, a touch on the shoulder may be all that is needed.

Remind them that we must give all children plenty of opportunities for praise.

Activity 3: Rewards 10–15 mins

Do you have a school policy of rewards? If so, perhaps this is the time to discuss and revise this. If not, perhaps this is the time to write one.

Make a group list of the rewards given to individual children in their class. These may include:

- golden time (time to choose what they will do)
- a 'well done' book (where comments are written in a book)
- name on a head's list, to be read out in assembly
- stickers
- increased responsibilities
- written comments on work
- a treat, for example, extra play, free choice or time on the PC
- a 'silver' letter or 'Good News' postcard to take home.

Alongside this list make a second list of rewards given to groups of children or to the whole class.

These may include:

- standing up in assembly for praise
- putting a marble in a jar for each good deed
- celebration assemblies involving parents and carers
- formal rewards; certificates or shields to groups
- prizes
- points
- half termly treats: disco, trip, film or video.

Activity 4: When to reward? 5–10 mins
Ask each participant in turn to give an example of when they reward a child. What has the child to do to receive a reward? Discuss each one and decide whether this is fair to all the children or whether only some children will ever receive rewards.

Final Activity 5: Involving children 2–3 mins
As a final part of this section ask the teachers to find out from their children what they would like to see as rewards for good work and behaviour. You could do this in Circle Time by asking each child to finish the sentence: 'Rewards for good work and behaviour I would like are…' Alternatively you could ask children to draw themselves receiving a reward for good work and to write what the reward is. Ask participants to bring this work to the next session.

Work with the children
Use the lesson notes and activity sheets on 'Praise and rewards' with the children before the next session.

Post programme Draw and Write
Do the Draw and Write again and analyse the children's responses before the next session. The instructions are exactly the same as for the pre-programme activity. Bring your results to the next session, numerical if you used the data collection sheet or relevant written responses from the children to facilitate a discussion.

Session 7   And finally...

Time   Min: 40 minutes   Max: 55 minutes

Focus on

- children's ideas about rewards
- working with children
- reflecting on the increase in self-esteem in children following the Draw and Write research strategy
- reflecting on the usefulness of these sessions.

Delay this session until at least the first five topics and activity sheets have been completed and the second Draw and Write completed and analysed.

Praise and rewards: 5 mins

Discuss the lesson and activity sheets on 'Praise and rewards' that you have done with the children since the last session.

Opening activity: 10 mins

Ask participants to tell the group what the children themselves would like to see as rewards. Jot these down on the flipchart. Discuss whether any of these ideas are feasible and whether they should replace those discussed in the previous session. Add any of these to those discussed last session and organise a printed list of rewards to be delivered to each participant to share with their class.

> **Preparation**
>
> Use PowerPoint **visual 10** below, or write on flipchart or OHP
>
> Help children to value themselves. Help them to:
>
> - think about what they are good at
> - give themselves praise for it
> - be proud of their own skills and achievements
> - talk to others they trust about how they are feeling
> - talk about things which they might find difficult
> - be good to themselves and treat themselves as special.

Activity 1: Valuing themselves 5–10 mins

Use **visual 10** or your flip chart and discuss ways to achieve the points listed there.

Activity 2: Children's responses from Draw and Write part 2 10–20 mins

Discuss these new second responses from the children. Highlight where children's self-esteem is improved and note any relevant phrases or expressions from the children. Where you have actual data figures, compare the before and after numbers. You may like to compare these on a class, school year or whole school basis.

Activity 3: Reflection 10 mins

This is the time to reflect on the whole programme. Discuss each phase of the programme with:

▶ the MDSs: has their interaction with the children improved?

▶ classroom assistants and other adults: how have they benefited from taking part?

▶ teachers themselves: has it enabled them to improve relationships with children with poor self-esteem?

▶ children; is there a new awareness of respect emerging in their relationships with each other and with adults?

Activity 3: Celebration

As a whole school, celebrate the completion of this programme. The children may have useful ideas for a whole school celebration!

Section 4 Lessons and activity sheets for children; an integral part of the adult training

These are the topics with activity sheets that are integral to the teachers' sessions.

topics	5–7 year olds	8–9 year olds	10–11 year olds
being positive	the bright side being an optimist	positive thinking turns out for the best	challenges half empty or half full
same, different and special	same and different we are all special	different talents what makes me special?	good points special gifts
feeling good	feeling good at school what makes us feel good?	skills confidence	valuing achievements enjoyment
communication	listening and speaking body language	presentation how I say it	what do I mean? speaking out
praise and rewards	praise me rewards for us	giving and accepting praise treating ourselves	taking pride celebrate

The bright side

Circle Time

Explain to the children that there are always two ways to look at things. You can look on the bright side and see what is good or you can look on the dark side and only see the things that are not so good. Give them an example from your own classroom, for example, you look on the bright side when you see all the good work that they do. Say that you sometimes look at children's work that is not so good and feel unhappy and then it is not so easy to look on the bright side. Ask them to finish the sentence: 'I look on the bright side when…' Jot down what they say.

Draw a picture

Ask the children to close their eyes and think of a time when something was not so good but they had the confidence to look on the bright side. Ask the children to draw a picture of this and to write how they managed to look on the bright side.

I was sad when I hurt my leg then I remembered it would be better in time for the holidays.

Missing Sam

Sam was a very friendly and popular boy in his class. He was always cheerful and really good at games. One day he told everyone that he was moving to a new house and school. Lots of the children were really sad and gloomy about this.

Ask the children to think of how they would feel if this was their class and Sam was their friend. How could they look on the bright side? What could they do? Make a list of what they could do.

Send a postcard

Give each child a postcard sized piece of paper with a line down the middle of one side. Ask them to draw on the blank side a picture of themselves missing Sam and on the other side to write a cheerful message to Sam about looking on the bright side. Ask them to make up the name and address of Sam's school to put in the address place.

Activity sheet

Explain that they don't need to use the words in the wordbox if they have others. The space in the wordbox is for you to write other words they might need in doing this work. Before the children start this, talk about ways to cheer yourself up if things go wrong. Talk about what to do when things go wrong, how to make things better and how to make sure you try not to make the same mistake again.

The bright side　　　　　　　　My name is......................

It is good to look on the bright side because

....

....

Write how you feel when you look on the
bright side and how you feel when you don't.

on the bright side	not on the bright side
I feel…	I feel…

Draw someone in your family looking on the bright side.	This is............................ They look on the bright side when...

Turn over the paper.

Draw a picture of yourself looking on the bright side when
something has gone wrong. Write about what went wrong and
how you cheered yourself up.

Being an optimist

Circle Time

Write the word optimist on the board. Explain to the children what this means. Ask them to think of words and phrases that could mean the same as optimist and jot these down in a list.

> **an optimist...**
>
> is cheerful
> looks on the
> sunny side
> keeps calm
> forgets
> mistakes
> doesn't worry
> will do better next time

Ask the children to think whether they are an optimist or not. Ask volunteers to tell the class of times when they think they were optimistic.

Tell a story

Azif was usually a cheerful boy; he was always full of fun and made people around him feel really good. Sometimes things would go wrong and he would feel bad for a moment or two but he would usually say something like 'Well, I won't make that mistake again.' or 'I guess I'll just have to try a bit harder next time.' Azif had lots of friends because he usually felt good about himself. He was a real optimist.

Ask the children to touch their ears if they think they are like Azif, cheerful and positive. Count how many. Ask the children to touch their nose if they are trying to be like Azif.

Draw a picture

Ask the children to draw a picture of Azif on a day when things go wrong. Is he smiling in their picture? How does he feel? Ask them to finish this sentence: 'I think Azif will…'

When things go wrong

Ask the children to think of a time when something went wrong and to think of what they did about it. Did they look on the bright side and make an effort to do better? Did they feel unhappy and cry? Does being unhappy and crying make things better? Ask volunteers to tell you what went wrong and what they did. Ask the children to work with a friend and make a list of the best thing to do if:

- they break something
- they spill something
- they make a mess
- someone is cross with them
- they hurt themselves or feel ill
- they make a mistake.

Share these responses as a class and decide the best things to do.

Activity sheet

Read the activity sheet with the children and explain what they have to do.

Being an optimist

My name is..................

It is good to be an optimist because

....

....

Draw a picture of you being optimistic. What are you doing?

I am...

Turn over the paper.

Draw two pictures. One where someone has made a mistake and feels bad about it. In the other draw someone making a mistake and being an optimist about it. Write about your pictures.

Positive thinking

Talk to the children about positive thinking. Ask them if they know what you mean with these two words. Ask a volunteer to jot down what the children say to make a list. Read through your list. Explain that some people are always positive and some people always negative but that most of us are part of each. Positive people usually have a happier and more fulfilling life because they seek to overcome obstacles instead of giving in.

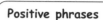

> **Positive phrases**
>
> Looking out for the best. Ignoring negative things. Looking on the bright side. Things will turn out OK. Not being downhearted. Being optimistic. Being cheerful. Thinking positively. Living in hope. Being constructive. Encouraging yourself.

Are you a positive person?

Ask the children to reflect on some of the things they have done lately; things at school and at home. Are t here times when they have acted in a positive and perhaps assertive way? Can they think of times when they have been negative? Ask the children for examples.

Use these phrases

Ask the children to work in pairs and write a sentence using one of the positive phrases on the list they made. Ask them to finish by writing two more sentences; how they think people feel when they are being positive and how they can feel when they are full of negativity.

Come together as a group and ask one from each pair to read out their sentences.

'I was positive when…'

Ask the children to finish this sentence and write it down. Ask them to write what led up to them being positive and what could have happened if they had been negative. Ask volunteers to share this work with the class.

Think of a story

Ask them to work with a different partner and think of a story they know where the hero or heroine has acted positively to achieve the result they want. Ask them to identify the part of the story where the main character seeks to do this. Ask them to think up an alternative scenario where the main character could have given in and acted negatively; how would the story have ended in that case? Allow ten minutes for this discussion and then ask for volunteers to tell the class.

Slogan

Ask the children to work in small groups and to write a slogan about being positive. Ask them to check the spelling and grammar and then to write it large in a speech bubble. Display these.

Activity sheet

Explain to the children what an agony aunt is. Read with them the letter and explain that they have to write a reply.

Positive thinking

My name is.................…...................

Dear Agony Aunt,

My friend always looks on the black side of life. It is making me feel unhappy about life as this person is so negative. We are going on a school trip soon and this friend keeps on about things going wrong. We will all be homesick, the food will be awful, we won't sleep well in the dormitory and that sort of thing. The teachers won't help. We'll have to do dangerous activity things. I just don't know how to handle this. Can you tell me what to say to this person, what to do and how to handle this negativity.

Yours faithfully,
Chris Doe

Dear Jo,

You could say to them….

You could do…

You could handle this by…

Turn over the paper.

Draw yourself on this school trip and write whether you take the advice, how you overcome the negativity that this person is making you feel. Write how the trip turns out for you and also for this friend.

Turns out for the best

Tell a story

Sareen wanted to go on the school weekend trip but her parents couldn't afford the money. She was really upset because she wanted to go with her friends. At first she was very miserable and so were her parents because they couldn't help her. The time came nearer and nearer and Sareen began to feel left out. The week before the trip a new girl, Josie, came into their class. She was too late to go on the trip and was feeling very left out of her new class. Sareen befriended her and they talked about what they would do when the class went on the trip without them. They were the only two who couldn't go. Josie invited Sareen to visit her for a sleepover that weekend and her parents were happy to let her go. They had a wonderful time. When they went back to school on the Monday they were firm friends. So it had all turned out well after all.

Ask the children if this kind of thing has happened to them; something that has disappointed them at first but turns out for the best in the end. Ask them for examples.

Explain to the children that sometimes when you look at things you see only the best and sometimes you see only the worst. Ask them if they have ever had something happen that seemed to be all bad but later they could see really good outcomes. Help them to understand that concentrating on the best instead of the worst can be a positive thing to do and will make their lives happier.

Turned out well

My mum lost her job and was really sad. Then went and helped out in a school. She liked it so much that she went on courses and then did training to become a teacher. She was really happy in the end.

Write a story

Ask the children to write a story about something that turned out well after all. Ask them to illustrate their story. Ask children who do this well if you can share their stories with the rest of the class; this will reinforce your point. Display some of the work.

Happenstance

Talk to the children about good things happening by accident. There are stories of chefs who have turned a cooking disaster into a triumph. Tell the children about the pudding Eton Mess which was originally a meringue pavlova that went wrong and so the chef put the broken meringue, cream and fruit into bowls making a delicious new sweet. Can the children tell you any instances such as this?

What could happen next?

Write these happenings up on the board: losing money, missing someone, breaking a leg, losing a pet. Ask the children to work in pairs and discuss each happening. Ask them to work out a happy solution. Discuss things turning out for the best.

Activity sheet

Explain to the children that they have to imagine each scenario and think of the best and worst outcomes in each situation.

Turns out for the best

My name is...

The worst thing is...	The best thing is...
You have to leave your home and move to a new area...	
You find a lovely dog and want to keep it but your parents make you take it to the police.	
Your family want you to join an after school club but you don't want to.	

Turn over the paper.

Think of a time when you have been disappointed when you couldn't do something. Write about what happened. Did you look for a positive outcome? If not, what could you have done better?

Challenges

Talk to the children about the challenges that you give them in school. Ask volunteers to say what the recent challenges have been. Talk about personal challenges and ask the children if any of them set themselves personal challenges outside school. Jot down any of these that the children suggest and discuss each one.

> **Personal challenges to:**
>
> - do homework without reminders
> - get stuff ready the night before
> - remember my PE and swimming kit
> - read at least one book a week
> - help more at home.

I will feel

As a whole class ask the children to think about how they will feel when they have completed one of their challenges. Ask them to show with their face and body how this will make them feel. Ask them to think about rewarding themselves when they have achieved their goal. Jot down the kinds of things they will do to reward themselves.

Why challenges?

Talk about the importance of setting themselves challenges and achieving their goals. Can they see that it will increase their self-esteem as they succeed every time? Discuss what life would be like if humans did not challenge themselves to learn, invent, achieve or just strive for better things. We might still live in caves!

Choose an achievement

Ask the children to work in pairs and think of some achievement made by our ancestors; perhaps a discovery, scientific breakthrough, medical cure, new transport or invention. Ask the children to use the internet and books to find out who achieved this, when and how it was achieved and the difference it made to everyday life of human beings. Ask them to write up an illustrated report of this achievement and to say how they thought the people felt on achieving it.

We will do this

Ask the children to work in pairs and discuss personal challenges. Ask each to:

- make a list of three personal challenges for themselves
- number them and put them in order of importance
- discuss whether they can take on these challenges at the same time or whether they should do just one before going on to the next
- put a time limit on achieving each one
- decide whether to share these with their families or keep them secret from them
- jot down what they will do to celebrate the completion of each challenge.

Activity sheet

Ask children to use the activity sheet for challenges discussed in the previous activity or seek new challenges. They can decide whether to take the activity sheet home to share with parents or whether to keep it secret.

Challenges

My name is...................................

Write down three challenges you are going to set for yourself.

challenge	steps to achievement	time scale
1st challenge is...		
2nd challenge is...		
3rd challenge is...		

Turn over the paper.

Write about:

- how you feel now you have set your challenges
- how you will feel when you are working on your first challenge
- how you will feel when you have achieved success.
  Write whether this success will have given you confidence and raised your self-esteem.

Half empty or half full?

Talk to the children about feeling positive and having an optimistic outlook on life. Discuss the kinds of people who look at a glass with water up to the half way mark and see this as half full and people who see it as half empty. Ask them to close their eyes and think what kind of a person they are. Ask the half full people to raise a thumb and the half empty people to touch their eyebrows. Discuss whether people always see the glass as the same measure or whether their optimism changes according to their situation. Ask them whether they think people can change; is it possible to train oneself to be more positive and optimistic?

Discuss

Ask the children to debate the following statements. Do they agree on one? Ask them to vote and count up the votes.

It's better to be optimistic and always look on the bright side and be positive.

It's better to be pessimistic and think of the worst that can happen and then you won't be disappointed.

Explain that if you go at things with a negative attitude you are more likely to fail than if you go at things with a positive attitude. Positive people are usually go-ahead, lively and interesting; negative people often have fewer friends as their attitude affects others.

Class song

Do the children know the tune to the Monty Python song *Always look on the bright side of life*? Ask them to work in small groups and make up some new words to go with the tune. Ask each group to nominate a singer to sing their words to the class. Vote for the best or amalgamate the words from several songs to make a really positive class song. Write out the words as a poster and ask children to illustrate it. Display this in your school where other people can see it.

Always look on the bright side of life

The optimist creed

Duplicate this from the copy in the Appendix or put on the whiteboard. Read and discuss it with the children and see if you can come up with your own class creed.

Write story endings

Give the children the following scenario. Ask them to write two endings, an optimistic one and a pessimistic one. Ask them to write a short discussion at the end about what they think they would have done if they had been Jonni.

Jonni was not very good at school work. She usually got poor marks and her parents were not pleased with her. One day she lost her school project work. Even though she searched for it she was sure she wouldn't find it…

Activity sheet

Read through the scenarios with the children and explain that they are to write what they think would be a good thing for each character to do.

Half empty or half full?   My name is.....................................

Read these scenarios and decide the best optimistic outcome for the character.

Harry was quite a good painter. He went to painting classes outside school and he was doing quite well. He really enjoyed painting but he was always disappointed when he had finished a painting and never thought them very good. His teacher thought one of them was rather special and she wanted him to let her enter it for a competition but Harry was afraid that people would think it silly and even laugh at it.	I think the best thing for Harry to do is…
Jazmin was new at the school and hadn't yet made any good friends. Her birthday was coming up and her mother wanted her to have a party or a sleepover. Jasmin wasn't happy about this. She said she didn't know anyone to invite and she wasn't sure she wanted people to come to her house. It would be an awful party, she was sure… And then she'd have to go to school and face the people there afterwards. 'Oh no,' she wailed, 'don't make me!'	I think the best thing for Jazmin to do is…

Turn over the paper.

Write some good advice to these characters. Write what you could say to them to make them feel positive and build up their self-esteem.

Same, different and special 5–7 year olds

Same and different

Circle Time activity

Ask the children to tell you the ways in which we are all the same. Ask them to finish the sentence; 'We are all the same because we…' Jot down what the children say and make a list. Remind them that even though we are all the same, we are all very different and all very special.

all the same

two eyes
two legs
hair
arms
hands
speak
eat
drink

Explain that there is no one in the world exactly the same as they are and that we are all unique. Ask them to close their eyes and think about how they are different and special from anyone else in the room. Ask them to finish the sentence, 'I am special because…'

Foods I like

Ask the children to think about the foods they like. Ask them to touch their nose if they like various foods, for example, eggs, cheese, meat, ice cream. Count those who like each item of food and jot down the number beside the food. Which foods do most children like? Which foods are least liked? Use this data to make a wall chart with each child making a small drawing of the food they like best and assembling their drawings as a chart. Add speech bubbles making sure that one of them is about us all being different and all liking different things.

Games I like

Ask the children to think about the games they like to play. Ask them to touch their elbows if they like various games, for example, football, ludo, snakes and ladders, computer games. Again count the numbers of children who like each game.

Ask the children to think of one way they are the same as someone in their family and one way that they are different from that same person. Ask them to draw this person, write the person's name and to write how they are the same and how they are different.

Work at home

Ask the children to find a photo of someone else in their family that they look like and find out the things that make people say that they look alike. What things make them different? Ask them to find out about the personality of this person. Is it the same as theirs?

Activity sheet

Help the children to understand how to do the activity sheet on the facing page.

Same and different   My name is.................................

Draw yourself, draw a friend.

How are you the same?

Me	My friend	We are the same....

Draw two children you know. How are they different?

Friend 1	Friend 2	They are different...

Turn over your paper.

Draw a line down the middle. On one part draw children who like to play the same games that you play. On the other part draw some children who like to play different games. Write about your drawings.

We are all special

Circle Time activity

Remind the children that we are all the same in some ways and all different in others. Explain to them that we are all special and really special to some people. Ask them to close their eyes and think of the people that they are really special to. Ask them to finish this sentence: 'I am special to...' Make a list of these people not by name but by relationship.

Read through the list and ask them to think what makes them special to these people. Ask them to finish the sentence; 'I am special to ... because...'

Make a list of all the reasons that people can be special, for example, because she loves me, because I am her child, because we are neighbours, friends.

> **We are special to…**
>
> our families
> our mums
> our dads
> my sister
> my gran
> the lady next door
> my dog
> friends
> brothers
> aunts and uncles.

Drawing activity

Ask the children to fold a paper into half and to draw two pictures of people that they are special to. Ask them to write the person's name on the paper and to say why they are special to this person.

How do you feel?

Ask the children to tell you how they feel when they are with these special people. Can they help you to make a list of all these feelings? Display these feelings words.

Who is special to me?

Ask the children to think of all their special people. Ask volunteers to write on the board the names or jobs of people who are special to them. After naming people close to them ask for other examples, such as the crossing patrol, the lady at the shop, the sports instructor. Celebrate that the children are special to all these people.

Drawing activity

Ask the children to choose one of the special people from the list and to draw a picture of that person. Ask them to write the name of the person and why they are special. Use these pictures to make a display of all the special people the children in your class know together with the writing about them.

Activity sheet

Read through the activity sheet and make sure the children know what they have to draw and write.

We are all special

My name is............................

Finish these sentences and draw.

I am special to my family because......

....

....

I am special to my friend.................. because........................

....

This is me being special to ....

Turn over the paper.

Draw all your special people and write their names. Write a sentence about each one. Use some of the feelings words.

Different talents

Circle Time

Ask the children to think of their talents; the things they are good at doing. Remind them that we are all good at some things and not so good at other things. Ask them to jot down a list of three of their talents. Ask a volunteer to jot these down on the board as a list as the children read out one from their list. When all the children have had a turn ask them to look at their list and if they have a talent that is not listed on the board to raise a hand and tell the writer. Examine the list of talents. Ask the children if they can put these in some kind of order, such as physical and mental or school and home, or learning and play. Celebrate with the children all the things that the children in your class are good at.

My strengths

Ask each child to work alone and write a list of all their strengths. Against each strength ask them to write about how they came to have this strength, for example, did they learn it or did someone teach them, did they choose to do this or did someone suggest it?

Challenges

Ask the children to think about the things they are not so strong in; things that challenge them; things they need to try to get better at. Ask the children to think about how they get better at various skills. Ask them to tell you what we have to do if we want to get better at things and make a list on the board. Talk through these things that the children have to do. Can they identify things that they must do to improve; things they need to work on?

> **To get better...**
>
> ask for help
> work out small steps or goals
> concentrate on one thing
> practise regularly
> ask people to monitor me
> tick off when one step is OK
> celebrate each goal achieved.

Personality strengths and weaknesses

Ask the children to think about the kind of person they are: their personality. Are they quiet or loud, impatient or patient, thoughtful or thoughtless? Ask each child to jot down an outline of their own personality and ask them to be very honest. Ask them to work with a partner and share their personality list. Can the partner suggest other strengths to add to the list? Ask the children to work alone, to draw a picture of themselves, list their strengths and write about their personality.

> I work hard at things and I don't like to get things wrong. I get cross with myself when I can't do things. I am not very patient and I hate it when people keep me waiting.

Activity sheet

Explain that you will want to read this work before the children take the sheets home. Ask the children to make sure they are honest in these responses.

Different talents

My name is.............................

Focus on your strengths and challenges. Finish the sentences.

I am good at   When I do this I feel
I am good at   When I do this I feel
I am <u>quite</u> good at   When I do this I feel
I am <u>quite</u> good at   When I do this I feel
I am <u>not yet</u> good enough at   To get good at this I must
I am <u>not yet</u> good enough at   To get good at this I must

Turn over the paper.

Draw two pictures.

One picture of you doing something you're really good at. Write what you had to do to become good at this.

Draw another picture, this one of your next challenge. How will you feel when you have achieved it?

What makes me special?

Introduce this topic by reminding the children that we are all different and special. Can you tell the children how you are special and whom you are special to?

Whom are you special to?

Talk about the people who think we are special. These will include our families, friends, relations neighbours, coaches, club leaders, teachers and so on.

I am special because…

Ask the children to think about their own special-ness. Ask volunteers to give you words for the different ways that they are special. Read through this list of special words and talk about each one.

> **I am special because…**
>
> I am tall
> I am good at football
> I could read when I was 4
> I am good at gymnastics
> I have learned to ride a bike
> I can bake scones
> I have learned to knit
> I grow things in the garden
> I can make a cup of tea
> I know how to dive.

My special people…

Talk about the people who are special to us. Talk about families who always support us even when things go wrong. Talk about friends and how they are there for us. Talk about people in the media who may be the children's role models. Remind the children that we have a responsibility to support our friends and to let them know that they are special to us. Ask the children to fold a paper into half and using both sides, to draw on one side, two people we are special to and on the other side to draw two people who are special to us. Ask the children to write who these people are and about their relationship with them.

How do I feel?

Talk with the children about how they feel when they are with their special people.

- How do they feel when things are going right for them?
- How do they feel when things are not going so right for them?
- What kinds of things do they do to keep these special people happy and to be happy themselves when they are together?
- Does being with these people make them feel confident and happy?
- Do they feel good about having these people as their special people?

When things become unsteady

Ask the children to think of the things they do to keep their relationship with these special people on an even keel. Sometimes things will go wrong between even special people. Talk about what you can do to get the relationship steady again. Do they, for instance, talk through the differences, make it easy for someone to say sorry, say they are sorry at once, find ways to help?

Activity sheet

Make sure that the children understand what they have to do. A robot has no feelings; they have to programme the robot to have feelings and understand about being special.

What makes me special?   My name is..

This is a robot that has just been invented.

This robot doesn't know about relationships and feelings and feeling special. Draw the robot and give it a name.

Write down all the things that you can tell the robot about being special...

Can you programme this robot? What kinds of things would you put in his memory bank to help him to understand about being special?

How would you programme it to make it understand the importance of fostering good relationships?

Turn over the paper.

Draw some of the people you are special to and write why you are special to them.

Draw two of the people who are special to you and write why they are special to you.

Good points

Remind the children that we are all different and that we are all special to our families and friends. Remind them that we have good points and not so good points. Remind them that we feel and behave differently on different occasions, in different places and according to how we feel that day. Sometimes our good points seem to disappear and we think only of the bad. Other days we feel really good and forget our failings.

Getting up

Ask the children to think of getting out of bed on a day when they feel really good. Ask them to give you words about these feelings. Jot these down to make a list. Ask them to think of the opposite; a bad day and how they feel then. Write a second list of these feelings. Look at the two lists. Ask the children to think how they can make sure they always have good feelings at the start of the day and not the feelings on the second list.

Turn it around

Ask the children how they can turn around a bad start to make it a good day. What kinds of things can they do to be good to themselves and make themselves feel ready for a good and positive day? How can they jerk themselves out of feeling bad and turn it into feeling good? Discuss what the children say. Write up any good advice.

My good points

Ask the children to write down four lists:

- their good points
- all the things they are good at
- what they like doing best
- how they feel when things are going well.

Ask them to take the lists home to share with their families.

Count your blessings

Remind the children to focus on these four lists. It would be a good idea to write them up somewhere at home and add to them as they get better at, and interested in doing other things. On a bad day they can look at this list and 'count their blessings'. Remind them to focus on the positive and not on things that they can't change, such as about their appearance.

Negative to positive

Ask the children to write a story of a day starting really badly, where the character felt negatively about everything. Then help the character in the story to begin to act more positively and turn the day around into a good one. Write about why the person felt bad in the first place and how they managed to change.

Activity sheet

Make sure the children don't use people's names. Ask them to concentrate on people who are very different from them, with different skills and attitudes.

Good points   My name is...

This activity sheet is about looking for good points in various people.
One of my friends has some really good points. They are...

One of my parents has some really good points. They are...

Someone else at home has really good points. They are...

A person I know really well outside school has really good points. They are...

Someone I look up to has really good points. They are...

Turn over the paper.

Think about someone who is well known in the media, press or sports world who has some kind of disability but strives for perfection in spite of this. Write who this person is and how they have managed to succeed even with their disability. Try to find out about this person's successes to include in your writing. The internet may help.

Special Gifts

Remind the children that we are all different and all special. Talk about people with special gifts; gifts, such as being a pianist, first class gymnast, wizard at maths or an artist. Talk about how these children have these gifts. Were they genetic? Were they the result of being in the right place at the right time? Were they because of parents' or carers' interests? Ask the children to give you names of some grown-up people who are famous because of these special gifts; discuss each one.

Our gifts

Explain to the children that we all have special gifts; it's just that some are more obvious than others and they may not have discovered theirs yet. The people they mentioned who have obvious gifts must have nurtured them and spent a lot of time practising the skills they need in order to succeed. Ask each child to think of some special quality, personal attribute or interest that they have; this could be their special gift. Ask volunteers to say what special talent or gift they have which may be almost within their grasp. Remind them to include personal qualities such as perseverance and patience. List these on the board.

> **Special gifts**
>
> thoughtfulness
> caring about others
> empathy
> being organised
> being reliable
> quick wittedness
> willingness
> nimble fingers
> strength
> creativity

Ask them to think about how to nurture these qualities and turn them into a gift.

What are yours?

Remind the children that everyone has such gifts or personal qualities although they may not always recognise them. Ask them to work in pairs and talk about their partner's gifts. Some people have lots of small gifts that make them the person they are. Ask them to consider carefully how to nurture these gifts and turn them to advantage. Ask each child to work alone and to write down any unpractised gifts they may have. Ask them to write alongside what they have to do to nurture these gifts.

Debate

Some people who are especially gifted in one area are lacking in awareness in others. For example, the absent-minded professor is no myth. If someone is really single-minded they are often not easy to know. Ask the children to debate these statements:

- It must be wonderful to have one great and special gift to use all your life.
- It is better to have several small gifts and use them to advantage.
- Having a rounded personality and being able to get on with people is better than being a genius at something.

Activity sheet

Ask the children to read all the way through the sheet before starting it. Explain that these gifts are part of their personality and reveal who they are. They should first finish the sentence and then put one or two ticks in the end boxes.

Special gifts

My name is..

My very special gifts or qualities are...

Mark the other special gifts or qualities you have.
Put one tick if you are working towards fostering that gift.
Put two ticks if you already have that gift.

I value myself.	
I know my strengths and weaknesses.	
I don't give up easily.	
I am good at working at relationships.	
I am a good communicator.	
I am good at handling pressure.	
I have the confidence to express my point of view.	
I can listen to and respect the point of view of other people.	
I am good at keeping promises.	
I can talk about my feelings.	
I am fairly creative.	
I am a good friend.	
I keep calm and can manage difficult situations.	
I can recognise risks and hazards.	
I know when and where to get help.	
I can maintain my own self-esteem.	
I can maintain and enhance self-esteem in others.	

Turn over the paper.

Write down one personal gift that you would really like to have. Write down why you want this gift and how you would use it. Write what you will have to do in order to obtain this gift?

Feeling good at school

I feel...
warm inside
as if I can do anything
on top of the world
great
confident smiling
brave
cheerful
clever.

Circle Time activity

Talk to the children about their feelings. Explain that sometimes we feel good about ourselves and sometimes we don't feel so good. Ask the children to think about their feelings they have when they are feeling really good about themselves. Where do they feel these feelings? How does it feel? Ask them to finish the sentence: 'When I feel good about myself I feel…'

Ask the children to think of what they can do to make other children at school feel good about themselves. Ask volunteers to tell you some of the things they do, such as, being friendly, praising them, admiring their work, saying they are good, asking them for help.

Ask the children to think about what they can do to make teachers, classroom assistants and other grown ups at school feel good. Ask volunteers to say what children can do to make grown-ups at school feel good, such as being cheerful, obedient, thinking of their feelings, being kind and helpful.

Draw a picture

Ask the children to draw a picture of themselves at school doing something that will help someone else to feel good about themselves. Ask them to write where they are in the picture, who the people are and what they are doing. You could display this work under the heading, 'Making others feel good about themselves'.

Coming to school

Ask the children to think of coming to school on a day when they feel really good about themselves. Ask them to work in pairs and write a list of all the things that make them feel good about coming to school on this day. Ask them to include on the way to school, waiting to come in, what they are going to do, people they will be with, play and dinner times, lessons they like.

Ask them to share their list with another four and make one list. Ask each child from the four to look at the list and think which of these things applies to them. Ask each of them to write four sentences about the things that make them feel good about coming to school. Ask them to take this work home to share with families.

Activity sheet

Help the children to read the words and to understand what they have to do.

Feeling good at school   My name is…………….......………

Children make me feel good about myself at

school when they……………………….......…

………………………………………………………

………………………………………………………

Draw a picture of a child at school helping you to feel good.

Turn over the paper.

Draw a picture of a grown up helping you to feel good at school.
Write what they are doing and how it makes you feel.

Feeling good 5–7 year olds

What makes us feel good?

Circle Time activity

Tell the children that you are feeling good today. Tell them some of the things that make you feel good in and out of school on this particular day.

Ask them to raise a thumb if they are feeling good today. Ask them to tell you one thing that makes them feel good. They can finish the sentence; 'I feel good today because…'

> **feeling good**
>
> sun shining
> outdoor play
> finished my book
> time to paint
> with a friend
> party today
> going out
> dad will meet me
> football after school

Jot down what they say and talk about all these things that make children feel good about themselves.

Draw a picture

Ask the children to draw a picture of them doing something that make them feel good at home. Ask them to draw the people they are with and to write under their picture about why they are feeling good. Use these pictures to make a class book or a wall display with the heading, 'These things make us feel good at home.'

When we don't feel so good

Talk about the days when you don't feel so good. What kinds of things makes you feel like this sometimes? What do you do about it? Ask the children to finish the sentence: 'When I don't feel so good, I…' Talk about the things that help us to stop feeling like this. Will these things work for everyone?

Feeling good about yourself

Talk to the children about feeling good about ourselves; the kinds of things that help us to know that we are special and unique. Ask volunteers to help you to make a list of the things they themselves can do to make them feel this way and talk about each one.

Ask children to think about what other people do or say to us that makes us feel like this, for example when someone praises us or when someone cheers us for something we have done. Make a second list. Talk about these lists. Are some things the same?

Work at home

Ask the children to talk to their families about the things that make people there feel good about themselves. Ask them to remember one of these things to tell the class.

Activity sheet

Explain the activity sheet to the children and make sure that they know the words and understand what they have to do. Encourage children to take theirs home to talk with their family about what they have drawn and written.

What makes us feel good?   My name is................................

Things that make me feel good are.................

....

....

I feel good about myself when someone says........

....

or...

wordbox
surprises
treats
birthdays
kind
people
playing
friends
well done
clever
tried.

Draw you feeling good about yourself.

Write what you are doing.

I am................................

....

....

....

....

....

Turn over the paper.

Draw yourself at home making someone there feel good. Write about your picture.

Feeling good 8–9 yr olds

Skills

Circle Time

Talk to the children about the skills they learned before they came to school; skills such as eating, walking, dressing themselves, leaning about good manners. Make a list of all these pre school skills. Talk about how they learned to do these things. Were they taught? Did they copy? Did they just find out for themselves?

Ask the children to focus on the skills they have learned since starting school; skills such as reading, writing, PE, history and geography. Talk about how they acquired these skills, your part as their teacher and their part as the learner.

Ask the children if they have ever taught another people a skill, for example, teaching a young sibling to read, teaching ball skills, showing how they do something so that someone can copy. Ask volunteers to tell you what they did.

Mastering a skill

Remind the children of all the things they have learned in these eight or nine years and how they felt as they mastered each skill. Ask volunteers to give you words that tell of their good feelings when they master a skill or move onto the next step of learning it. Ask each child to draw themselves mastering a skill and to write how they felt when they had achieved this.

When I swam a width of the pool I felt really proud of myself. So did my mum and my brother.

More skills

Remind the children that all through their school life and beyond they will have to learn new skills, practise them and master them. Explain that we are never too old to learn new things. Ask them to think about the grown-ups they know and whether any of these have been learning new skills. Ask volunteers to tell the class about these.

When I am grown up

Ask the children to tell you of the skills they want to learn when they are grown up; skills such as driving a car, becoming a sportsperson, a doctor or learning to do other work. Ask each child to draw a picture of themselves doing this. Ask them to write about how they will learn to do it and how they will feel when they have learned to do it. You could make a display of these pictures to show to parents on their next visit.

How I feel

Remind the children of the good feelings they have when they have learned to do something new. Learning new skills and being able to teach people to do things gives us confidence to go on and learn more.

Activity sheet

Explain that the children have to reflect on the skills they have already learned.

Skills

My name is...

This is a drawing of what I learned	This is how I learned to do it.
When I was one I learned to	
When I was two I learned to	
When I was four I learned to	
When I was six I learned to	
Last year I learned to	

Turn over the paper.

Write down the next thing you want to learn to do. Write down what you will need so that you can learn to do it and how you will feel when you can do it.

Confidence

Ask the children to work in pairs, find out and jot down what the word confidence means. Give them only five minutes. Come together as a class and write on the board what they have found out.

Read through their definitions. Ask the children to think about whether they feel like this; all the time, sometimes, occasionally, never. Ask the children to think about how they can increase their self-confidence and the kinds of things that will bolster their confidence. Ask volunteers to finish the sentence 'I would have more self confidence...'

> **confidence means...**
>
> being able to do things
> being assured
> being cool
> self-reliant
> self-assured
> feeling good about yourself

Speaking out

Ask the children to work in pairs and to think of their strengths. Using these strengths, ask each one to say to the other: 'One of my strengths is… I know I am good at this.' Ask them to change over and then think of another strength so they will have two affirmative statements. Ask each pair to join up with another pair and to say quietly and firmly their two statements. Ask the children to remember these affirmations and to say them firmly and confidently to their mirror at home. Remind them that the more they affirm their confident statements the stronger and more confident they will feel.

New affirmations

Talk to children about what they want to achieve, what skill they want to learn, what they want to get better at. Once they have stated this privately to themselves it is possible to break it down into small steps goals. Ask each child to work alone and decide on the skill they want to achieve or perfect. Ask them to write down this skill and think of the steps they will have to take to achieve it. Ask them to number the steps. The first thing to do is to make a personal affirmation, such as 'I am going to learn to… and I will reach the first step on… (date)' Ask the children to keep their personal affirmation private but to take it home and to read it firmly and confidently every evening until they have reached the first step. Then it is time for celebration and the start of the next step. Ask the children to keep a log of their progress. Ask volunteers to discuss their progress.

Showing confidence

Ask the children how people can tell if someone is confident. Can they give you words and phrases that can be used about people who are confident, for example, they stand tall, look you in the eye, listen to you, have strong body language and so on. Using these attributes ask the children to role play someone who is confident. Ask them to walk or sit showing that they have confidence. Now ask them to think of how people who are not confident look. Can they give you a list of words to describe them? Discuss what we have to do so that we can look and feel confident.

Activity sheet

Explain to the children what they have to do on this sheet. They can take it home.

Confidence

My name is...

Draw here	Write here
This is a confident person	You can tell this person is confident because
This person is not confident	You can tell this person is not confident because

Turn over the paper.

Draw yourself doing something in which you are confident. Write what you are doing and how people can tell that you are confident.

Valuing achievements

Talk to the children about recognising their achievements in school. Some children are unable to realise what they do achieve and they must be made aware of when they have achieved something and value this. Ask the children to tell you what they have achieved during the past term in your class. Make a list of all these achievements. Did you celebrate these? How did you do that? Help the children to realise that by valuing what they achieve they can feel good about their school work and it will spur them on to achieve more. This is like a wheel of success.

A wheel of success

Ask the children to make a wheel of success of one of their achievements. You might choose some whole class success and ask them all to do the same or you may prefer to ask them to work in pairs or small groups on individual successes. It should turn out to be similar to the self-esteem triangle. Children need to write what and how they did it under similar headings to those in the diagram.

Write a report

Talk about really sensational achievements; a yachtsman circumnavigating the globe, a climber conquering a peak, a trek across barren country. Can they invent a similar sensational achievement and write a report for a newspaper about the fictitious team or person who has achieved this success. Ask them to make sure to include the feelings of the person or team at all stages of the occurrence, for example, fear of failure, wanting to give up, being spurred on. Write also how the world's press would help this person or team to celebrate as well as how the individuals would do this.

What lifts you up?

Ask the children to think about the things they do to make themselves feel good if they feel down or unhappy. You could ask them to finish this sentence; 'When I need cheering up, I…' Make a list of these things such as listening to music, doing something energetic, watching TV or video, eating or reading a book. It may, or may not, include talking to someone about it. Discuss each of the children's responses and how doing this makes them feel better. Ask the class to identify the responses on the list that make the most sense and are the healthy choices we can make when we need cheering up.

Role play

Ask the children to work in pairs with one of them needing cheering up and the other offering advice to help them to cheer up. Change over. Ask volunteers to show their role play to the class. Ask them if doing this kind of role play helps them to think of new ways to make themselves feel good when they are down?

Activity sheet

Explain that Sam can be a girl or boy. They have to write a reply to this letter as if they were the agony aunt giving advice to Sam about how to value achievements.

Valuing achievements

My name is.....................................

This is a letter written by a pupil in your class. This person seems really unhappy and under-achieving. If you were the agony aunt what advice would you give to them?

Dear Agony Aunt,
I am really fed up. I don't seem to be any good at anything. My friends are all getting on OK and seem happy at school but I don't seem to be able to get on at all. Our teacher keeps on about valuing achievement but I don't seem to have any achievements to value. I feel so worthless. What can I do?

Sam

Dear Sam,

Turn over the paper.

Think about the advice you gave to Sam. Write about what happens when Sam takes your advice. Write a happy ending for Sam.

Enjoyment

Ask the children to think about the things that give them enjoyment, such as sport, going out with friends or being creative. Ask each child to contribute by finishing the sentence: 'I get enjoyment from…' Jot down their responses and as a class consider the list. Are they about:

- fun things they do
- being with people and laughing together
- doing things
- being on your own
- learning or practising skills?

Ask the children to group the responses under various headings.

We enjoy…

making things
playing with friends
playing computer games
being outdoors
in the country
gardening
woodwork
going on my bike
swimming
listening to music.

What do you enjoy?

Ask each child to draw a picture about doing one thing that they really enjoy doing. It can be at home, school or somewhere else. Ask them to write about why they enjoy doing this activity and the history of doing it, for example, when they started, whether they needed help, whether it is ongoing and something they will carry into later life, whether it is active or passive, a skill or a hobby. Display some of this work with speech bubbles naming the pastimes. Ask the children to suggest a heading, for example 'Life is enjoyable'

How does it make you feel?

Talk to the children about how they feel when they are doing this one thing that they enjoy so much. Ask volunteers to give you feelings words. Ask each child to choose one feelings word to write up large in a speech bubble to add to the display of their work. Ask the children whether these feelings words show that they feel confident and with good self-esteem when they are doing these things that they enjoy.

Group work

Ask the children to debate these two statements in their groups and decide if either is strictly true. Can they write an alternative which they all agree on?

You only really enjoy things if they are easy and you don't have to work at them.

You only really enjoy things if you have had to put some effort into learning how to do them.

Write up any alternative statements that the children come up with. As a whole class can you choose one or amalgamate their statements to make one that the children all agree to?

Activity sheet

Children are asked to list all the things that they enjoy and to say why they enjoy them.

Enjoyment

My name is...

Think about all the things that you enjoy. Think of the senses that you use when you are enjoying doing, seeing, playing with these things.

what I enjoy	why I enjoy it	how I feel	the senses I use

Turn over the paper.

Read through all the feelings words you have written on this side. Are they all words about feeling confident and good about yourself because you are enjoying something? Are any about achieving something? Draw yourself doing one of these things and write about it. How would you feel if you were suddenly unable to do this thing ever again?

Listening and speaking

Circle Time activities

Tell the children that you are thinking about communication in this lesson and that listening and speaking are ways that we communicate with other people. Ask them to think about listening and how hard it is to listen carefully sometimes. Can they think of times when they have found it hard to listen carefully? Ask them to finish the sentence: 'It's hard to listen carefully when…'

It's hard to listen when…

the TV is on
people are playing about
it's noisy
I want to play
people are outside playing
I sit at the back
someone interrupts
my friend is talking
someone is fidgeting.

Ask the children to think about how they show they are listening. How does their face look? Where are their eyes looking? Is their body still or moving?

Remind the children that it is important to listen. Ask them to finish the sentence: 'It is important to listen because…' Make a list of their responses. These will probably include: we might miss something, we could do the wrong work, we might not know what to do. Make a chart of these responses to display and to remind the children that it is important to listen.

Drawing activity

Ask the children to draw a picture of them listening to a story that you have read to them. Ask them to write a little of the story and to say why they enjoyed it.

Talking

Remind the children of the times when it is their time to talk and when it is not time to talk. Ask them to work with a partner and to write two lists; when to talk and when not to talk. Ask them to share these lists with another pair and then with the whole group.

Taking turns with a timer

Ask the children to work in pairs; give each child a letter, A or B. Ask them to talk about a subject you give them, for example, games we like. Explain that they have to take turns to talk and that when they hear the timer the person speaking has to stop and the other person talk. Ask the As to start. Use the timer after a minute. Change over so that each has two turns to talk. Back in the group ask the children to tell you how it felt to have to take turns like that. Did it help them to know that there is a time to talk and a time to listen? Would they rather talk or listen? Why?

Activity sheet

Read this with the children and help them to understand what to do.

Listening and speaking

My name is.....................

It's important to listen because...

wordbox
miss
things
understand
know
what
fair
hear
say

It's important to talk because...

It's important to take turns because...

Draw a picture of you talking with some friends in the playground.

Turn over the paper.

Draw yourself listening to someone at home. Write who you are listening to and what they are saying.

Body language

Circle Time activities
Explain that as well as listening and talking we communicate with our bodies. Ask the children to show you these faces:

- I'm happy today
- I don't understand
- I'm worried
- I'm scared
- I don't care.

Ask them to think about how they show these messages to other people with their faces. Do they know they can use their bodies as well?

How do I feel?
Demonstrate how you stand and look when you are really pleased with the children. Ask them to guess how you feel.

Demonstrate other body language and ask the children to guess, for example, being really excited with them, being sad, being cross, and so on. Explain that body language and what our faces say is just as important as the words we use.

Mime it
Write on the board: Happy, Worried, Excited. Ask the children to volunteer to stand in the circle and show one of these expressions using body and face. After three or four children have had a turn, group the children in pairs and ask each one to try to communicate without using their voices at all. Ask the children to start with the three expressions and one of each pair to demonstrate one of them with their partner having to guess. Come together and talk about whether it is easy to guess how people are feeling by their body language.

Draw a picture
Use the same three feelings as above and ask the children to draw themselves in these different ways, drawing their faces and bodies. Ask them to write about how they feel in their pictures and why they are feeling this way. Display some of these with a heading suggesting that we communicate with our faces and bodies as well as words.

Activity sheet
Read the activity sheet with the children. Remind them that it is about body language and how we communicate with parts of our bodies. Explain that people who are good communicators usually have confidence and high self-esteem.

Body language

My name is.....................

We can say things with our.............................

We can say things with our.............................

It's important to watch body language
because…

wordbox
faces
bodies
eyes
shoulders
stand
mouths
how
smile
grin

Draw a picture of someone you
know who is really happy. How
can you tell they are happy?

I can tell they are happy
because…

Turn over the paper.

Draw someone in your family
who is excited today. Write
how you can tell they are
excited. Write about why they
are excited.

Presentation

Discussion

Talk about the way that children present their work. Ask them to think about the various styles of work that children produce, for example, neat and well written, tidy and small, flowing and artistic, slapdash and untidy. Ask the children to discuss these statements and vote on which they think is the most true. Ask volunteers to say why.

1. You can tell that people are confident by the written work they do.
2. You can't tell anything about a person by written work.

Organisation

Ask the children how they plan letter writing. Do they think out the whole letter and decide how to present it? Do they dash it off just as it occurs to them? Do they write a draft and then copy it out? Discuss these and any other options that the children suggest. Help them to understand that a confident person may use any of these methods but that the finished letter will be well written with correct spelling and punctuation.

Presenters

Ask the children to think about various people who come to schools to talk to children about their work or leisure occupations. Explain that some of these people will be experts at talking to children while others may just be experts at talking about their subject. Ask the volunteers to tell you some of the preparation they think that these people will do before they come to school. Make a list of their suggestions.

> **They will...**
>
> prepare the talk
> practise reading it
> organise visual aids or charts
> select artefacts
> wear appropriate clothes
> locate the venue
> plan their route
> work out a timetable
> think about questions.

Presenting

Ask the children to work in small groups and select a topic that they would like to present to the class. Ask them to make a list of the things they need in order to present this topic. Ask them to plan what they will say and how they will say it. Ask them to think of the organisation of the room, where they will stand or sit. Ask them to organise how they will share the presenting task within their group.

Speaking

Ask the children to talk in their group about how they will speak to the class. How will they present a confident persona to the rest of the children? Ask them to list the things that will help them to look and feel confident, for example, practise before a mirror, stand square and look people in the eye, take a deep breath before starting, smile.

Ask a volunteer group to present their topic each week.

Activity sheet

Explain that this is about how they want people in various situations to see them.

Presentation

My name is.............................

Write about how you would like to present yourself to various people.

This is how I want to present myself to people in my family.	
This is how I want to present myself to my friends.	
This is how I want to present myself to important people.	
This is how I want to present myself to the head teacher at school.	

Turn over the paper.

Write a few sentences about how you feel inside when you are with the above groups of people. Write about how you would speak to these various people.

How I say it

Discussion

Talk to the children about how people communicate when speaking. Do they always think about what the words they are using? Do they always make sure they convey the meaning they wish? How can we make sure that people understand the meaning behind what we are saying? Ask volunteers to contribute to this discussion and end with a discussion of these two statements:

1. It's always better to think carefully before we speak.
2. It's better to just say what you mean without too much thinking about it.

Ask for a vote on these two sentences; allow children to abstain. Count how many children voted and how many abstained. Ask volunteers to say why they made their choice.

The words we use

Ask the children to think about the words that people use. Ask them to work in small groups and write down their responses and reasons, to the following questions:

- If people have time to prepare a statement will they use different words than if they are speaking in conversation? Why?
- Is it ever necessary to use swear words? Why?
- Does using 'bad language' mean that people have a small vocabulary? Why?
- Is the language on TV a reflection on the language we use in every day life?
- Why do they use text-speak on mobiles? Will complete words become obsolete?

Ask each group to prepare written responses to these five questions and elect a spokesperson to give their responses to the class. Discuss these responses.

The tone of voice

Ask the children whether they think the tone of voice is important in conversation. Talk with the children about how people can sometimes say outrageous things with a twinkle in their eye and a light hearted tone of voice that changes the message being delivered. People can also say kind words in a cold fierce voice that belies the truthfulness of the statement. Ask the children to work in pairs and jot down two or three sentences they could say in different tones of voice that alter the meaning. Ask volunteers to read their sentences to the group.

Confident delivery

Ask the children to think of how they present themselves when they are speaking to various people. Do they have a confident body language? Do they take a deep breath and stand tall before they start? Discuss how people can they make sure they control their feelings when in a difficult or worrying situation.

Activity sheet

The activity sheet reinforces the previous discussion.

How I say it

My name is...............................

Think of the different ways that you speak to various people and in different situations.

Draw yourself	Write about words you use and how you speak
with friends in the playground	In the playground I...
with my family at home	At home I...
to my teacher in the classroom	To my teacher I...
when I speak in Assembly	In Assembly I...

Turn over the paper.

Write an explanation of why you speak differently on different occasions.

What do I mean?

Communication is only effective if people really understand what you mean. Talk to the children about making sure that people understand the meaning of the words they are saying. We wouldn't talk to babies or young children using long words and complicated sentences. We wouldn't talk to important people using baby talk. Ask the children to think of the communication skills they need when talking to various people. Ask them to complete this sentence: 'When I talk to… I use …. words and phrases, for example…' Change the sentence to speaking on the phone or texting. Discuss what the children say and whether this is appropriate language to use in these particular circumstances.

> When I talk to the minister in the church I use respectful words and phrases, for example, 'I am sorry that I shall have to be late for choir practice. It's because my Dad can't take me until he gets home'.

Body language

Remind the children about their body language which is just as important as the words they use. Ask them to think of how someone's body would look in these situations:

- playing with friends
- after a sports session
- with their parents
- with an adult they don't know very well
- with a policeman after doing something anti-social
- when they are stopped by someone asking the way
- when they are being interviewed for a job.

Write about it

Ask the children to choose one of the above situations and to write a scenario which tells about the situation, what people said, how they said it and the body language of all the people involved.

The importance of punctuation

Explain that punctuation is essential when writing down what you mean. Ask the children to talk about the two meanings of the following identical sentences.

1. The teacher said, 'This boy is a genius.'
2. 'The teacher', said this boy, 'is a genius'.

Ask the children to work in pairs and to write pairs of sentences similar to those above, using the same words but with different punctuation that changes the meaning.

Share these sentences as a class. Discuss whether the change in meaning could be disastrous or merely funny.

Activity sheet

This activity will help children to view the meaning beyond the words used.

What do I mean?   My name is...

Put these phrases into everyday language that is easily understood by foreigners. Then think up a couple of your own.

what it says	what it means
trespassers will be prosecuted	
a stitch in time saves nine	
parking is limited to 20 minutes	
you need to pull your socks up	
a bird in the hand is worth two in the bush	
take that grin off your face and stand up straight when you are talking to me	

Turn over the paper.

Choose one of the above phrases and illustrate it. Write about what is happening.

Speaking out

Remind the children that they are thinking carefully about communication, saying what you mean and making sure that people understand the meaning of what they are saying. Explain that there will be times in their lives when they have to speak in front of other people. Children with good self-esteem will find this easy; those with low self-esteem will find this a daunting experience.

Small steps

A pupil from the school council has been asked to speak to the whole school on some relevant topic, for example, children arriving at school late or any other relevant topic. This pupil has to decide:

Small steps
choose keywords
write keywords on cards
display the poster
stand on the stage boxes
practise delivery.

- what to say
- how to remember what they are going to say
- whether they need any visual aids
- how and where to stand
- their delivery, that is pitch and tone of voice.

Ask the children to work in small groups to discuss this and then to write down what the pupil is going to say and the rest of the above steps. Ask them to choose a spokesperson to share this work with the rest of the class.

Diction

Explain that, when speaking to a large audience, it is essential to speak clearly and loudly. It is important to speak more slowly than usually and with careful pronunciation. Children who can do this will be those with self confidence and self assurance. In a large space, such as the hall, ask the children to work in pairs and to role play the above speaking activity. Can the listener hear and understand what the speaker is saying? Choose several self assured people for the whole class to listen to. Ask them all to practise speaking clearly and carefully at home in front of a mirror so that when they have to speak in an assembly they will be prepared.

Speak out!

Ask the children to think of times when people have to speak up against something that is happening. Ask them to give examples, such as facing up to bullies; saying what you know is right in spite of opposition; being brave to contradict someone. Remind them that they must not put themselves in danger but that free speech is everyone's right in this country. Ask the children to work in small groups to first discuss and then write a scenario where it is important for someone of their age to speak out. Ask one spokesperson from each group to read their scenario. Discuss each one with the whole class.

Activity sheet

This is about public speaking and also about speaking out. Remind the children not to put themselves in danger when speaking out.

Speaking out   My name is...

Think of one occasion when you had had to speak in public at school, in assembly, in drama or at home. Write how you prepared yourself for this task and how you felt before, during and after you had to speak.

The occasion was…

I prepared myself by…

Before it, I felt…

During it, I felt…

After it, I felt…

Think of an occasion, in a story or on TV, when someone had to speak out because something was happening that shouldn't. Write a brief description of the scenario before, during and after the person spoke out.

Turn over the paper.

Draw a scene from the above scenario. Write down what you would have said and done if you had been involved in the above action. How would you have made sure you were safe in doing this? If you felt in danger what other action could you have taken?

Praise and Rewards 5–7 year olds

Praise me!

Circle Time activity

Explain to the children the meaning of the word 'praise'. Ask them to think about when people praise them. What kinds of things do people praise them for? Ask them to finish the sentence: 'People praise me when…'

Mrs Jones smiles and says well done when I do good writing.

Ask the children to think of all the various people who do praise them at home. Ask them to touch their nose if they can think of someone who has praised them today. Ask them to finish the sentence: '…………………… at home, praises me when I…'

Who praises at school?

Ask the children to work in pairs and to make a quick list of the people who praise them at school. Alongside the list ask them to write about the things that people at school praise them for. Ask them to share their lists with another pair and then to share their list with everyone. Make a class list of all the people who praise children in your class and a second list of all the things that they are praised for. Display the lists.

Draw a picture

Ask the children to draw a picture of someone at school praising them for doing something well. Ask them to write what they are doing and who is praising them. How does the person praising them do it? What do they actually do or say?

How do people praise you?

Ask the children to think of the different ways that people praise children. Can you make a list of these ways? Your list may include:

- saying things such as 'well done'
- saying things about work; 'this is good work, you have tried'
- telling other people about good behaviour
- smiling at you
- touching your arm and saying something kind.

How do you feel?

Ask the children to tell you how they feel when they are praised, for doing something or for their behaviour. Ask volunteers to give you feelings words to say how they feel. Write these up on the board to make a list. Can you put them in some kind of order?

Activity sheet

Explain that the children have to finish the sentences before drawing a picture and writing about it. Ask them to share these with their families at home.

Praise me!

My name is...........................

Finish these sentences:

When people praise me at school I feel..............

....

....

wordbox
proud happy big important good full of it thankful warm

The last time I was praised at home was when ....

....

....

The best kind of praise is..

....

This is me praising someone	This is what happened...

Turn over the paper.

Draw yourself the last time you were praised by your teacher. Write about what you had done and what your teacher said or did to praise you.

Rewards for us

Explain to the children what a reward is. That it is a kind of praise for doing something good, thoughtful or clever. Explain that there are different kinds of rewards; sometimes people are rewarded with money if they find a lost cat or dog. Ask volunteers to tell you what kinds of rewards they know about.

Tell a story

Wahchi is seven years old and one day he is walking along the path to the shops with his mum when he sees something glinting in the gutter at the edge of the pavement; it's a keyring with two keys on it. His mum doesn't see them, so Wahchi points them out to her. She picks them up and looks around to see if anyone is nearby who might have lost them. No one is around. 'What shall we do Mum?' says Wahchi. They take them to the police station and hand them in to the officer on duty. The officer fills in a form with their names and addresses and says he will let them know. That evening, there is a ring at the doorbell and when Wahchi opens the door an old man is there. He has lost his keys and been to the police station. He is so glad that Wahchi and his mum handed in the keys that he gives Wahchi a reward; a five pound note!

Ask the children if they think Wahchi did the right thing. Did he deserve a reward? Did he hand the keys in so that he would get a reward?

Draw a picture

Draw Wahchi at his house when the man comes to thank them for handing in the keys. Write what the man said, what happened next and how Wahchi felt when he knew he had helped the man. How did he feel when he got the reward?

I think the man was grateful that Wahchi handed in the keys. I think Wahchi was glad too. He felt really happy with a reward.

Remind the children that we don't always get a reward when we do something good. Sometimes it is enough to know that we have done something that we should do.

Rewards at home

Talk with the children about rewards at home. What kinds of things do their families do to celebrate or reward people in the family when they have done something really good or special? Do they go out to celebrate; do they stay in and have a special meal? Ask volunteers tell about ways their families reward people.

Activity sheet

Help the children to understand the list they have to write on the other side of the paper.

Rewards for us

Write down the ways your teacher rewards children in your class.

wordbox

write
work
say
clap
stickers
smiley faces
whole
class
headteacher

Write down the ways that your school rewards children for doing well.

Turn over the paper.

Draw someone in your school being rewarded for doing something well. Write what they did. Think of other ways to reward children and make a list of them.

Giving and accepting praise

Ask the children to think of words that explain how they feel when someone praises them. Ask volunteers to tell these words and make a list on the board. Discuss each one. Put the words into two categories; one about feeling good and the other about feeling embarrassed. Ask children if they find it difficult to accept praise. Do some of the children find it hard to know what to say?

> **When I am praised I feel…**
>
> pleased
> excited
> warm inside
> comfortable
> happy
> go red
> embarrassed
> uncomfortable
> self-conscious.

Write about it

Ask the children to think of an occasion when someone praised them in school and how they felt about it. Ask each child to draw a picture of him/herself on this occasion. Ask them to explain the situation and write how felt both when they were being praised and when they thought about it or told their family afterwards. Discuss what the children have written. Do you need to give some of them advice about accepting praise graciously? Explain that a smile and a 'thank you' is a good way to act and that saying words that show embarrassment such as 'Don't be silly!' or 'It was nothing.' can be a way of putting themselves down.

Generous with praise

Ask the children if they ever praise other people's efforts or work. There must be occasions when people in class are praised; do other children reinforce this? Do they see the need to praise their friends on occasions? Can they see that praising other people enhances not only that person's self-esteem but also their own? Ask the children to recall times when they have praised someone in their family. Have they, for example, praised someone for cooking a meal, for repairing something, for cleaning something, for doing something well? Ask volunteers to tell the class about times when they have praised someone in their family.

Do more of it

Ask the children to work in small groups and discuss times when they can praise others both in and outside school. Ask them to jot down a list of occasions and situations when they can praise someone. Come together as a class and talk about all these situations.

Practise it

Ask the children to work in pairs and practise praising each other. They can use one of the occasions or situations in the previous activity and dramatise it. Make sure they change over roles and situations. Ask them to make sure they sound sincere and that they really mean the praise they are giving. Can some of the pairs show their role play to the class?

Activity sheet

Ask children to be truthful in this work. Ask them to take it home after you have seen it.

Giving and accepting praise   My name is...............................

True or false?

	True or false?
I get praised a lot.	
I have not been praised for a long time.	
Being praised at school gives me a good feeling.	
When I am praised at home I feel really happy.	
I get embarrassed when people praise me.	
I never think about praising other people.	
I praise other people a lot.	
I never know what to say when people praise me.	
When I praise people I feel confident and have good self-esteem.	

Turn over the paper.

Draw a picture of you being praised for some achievement. Write about who praised you, how you were praised and how it made you feel.

Praise and rewards 8–9 year olds

Treating ourselves

Talk with the children about how they treat themselves. Ask them if they reward themselves when they have done something well, behaved well or resisted temptation.

We all know, inside us, when we have done something to be proud of and we should celebrate that. Ask volunteers to tell you of their feelings when they have something to be proud of. Talk about each contribution. Now ask the children how they reward themselves when they know they have done something good and worthy. Jot down what they say. Can others add to the list? Remind the children that it's important to know when we have done something really good and to reward ourselves.

> **How I reward myself**
>
> smile inside
> have some chocolate
> tell my parents
> write to my gran
> phone a friend
> buy myself something
> read a comic
> stay up late
> watch TV
> play on the computer
> write it in my diary.

Write about it

Ask the children to think about the last time they did something that they were proud of. Ask them to write about what happened and how they felt. Ask them to write down any reward they gave themselves. If they didn't reward themselves, ask them to think about what they could have done.

Something not so good

Ask the children to reflect on times when they know they have not done their best, behaved badly, hurt someone's feelings, been unappreciative or bad tempered. Ask them to think about how they felt afterwards and how they treated themselves on that occasion. Ask the children to concentrate, not on what happened, but on what they did afterwards. Did they try to put it right? Did they apologise? Did they show that they were sorry in some way? Ask volunteers to tell you the kinds of things that they could do if something had gone wrong and they wanted to make amends.

Discussion

Ask the children to discuss these three statements. Are they right or wrong? Can they write a better statement?

1. When you have done something that has not been your best or when you have behaved badly you should always apologise to someone and yourself.
2. When you have done something that has not been your best or when you have behaved badly you should just forget it and get on with things.
3. When you have done something that has not been your best or when you have behaved badly you should reflect on it and make sure you don't make the same mistakes again.

Sing it

Ask groups of children to think of the song *Whenever I feel afraid, I whistle a happy tune* and compose a song to this tune about rewarding oneself when we do things well.

Activity sheet

The children finish the sentences and write how they treat themselves.

Treating ourselves   My name is...

Finish these sentences:

When I've done well at school I feel...

and I treat myself by...

When I've done something well at home I feel................................

and I treat myself by...

When I do well in tests, I feel...

and I treat myself by...

When I do well in our of school clubs I feel.................................

and I treat myself by...

When my teacher praises me I feel..

and I treat myself by...

When our whole group has done good work we feel.........................

and we treat ourselves by...

Turn over the paper.

Draw yourself receiving a sticker, reward or award from your school. Write about what you received, what you did to receive it and how you feel about it.

Taking pride

Talk with the children about the words pride and proud. What do they really mean? Jot down the words they tell you.

Talk to the children about this kind of pride, when people feel they are too good, too important and superior to others. Ask it this is a quality to be admired? Is this what we are asking children to strive for?

Pride

arrogance
conceit
smugness
superiority
over confidence
self importance
big headed.

The other kind

Ask the children to discuss these two statements.

1. *Take pride in your work.*
2. *Be proud of your achievements..*

These have almost the opposite meaning. Being proud of work and achievement is a good quality. Knowing that you have done your best makes you feel good about yourself and gives self confidence. This kind of pride is something to celebrate.

Differentiate

Ask the children to work in pairs and to invent two scenarios that illustrate these two different versions of pride; the bad quality and the good. Ask one of each pair to write up one of the scenarios, the other to write up the other.

Ask volunteers to read their scenario to the whole class and discuss whether the meanings of the words 'proud' and 'pride' are clear.

Pride in your work, accepting praise

Remind the children that to take pride in work, to do it to one's best and to feel good about the result is the kind of pride we want children in your class to have. They don't need to become conceited about it or to be big headed. So how can they accept praise for their work without becoming conceited? Ask the children to think of the kinds of things that people say when their good work is acknowledged and they are praised. Ask volunteers to give you words or phrases that would be good to use to acknowledge praise without giving the appearance of them being big headed.

The last time

Ask the children to think of the last time someone praised them. Can they remember the incident? What kind of impression did it make on them? Was the praise justified? How did they respond? Ask each child to write about this incident and to say how they were praised; who said or did what. Ask them to stop here and to consider the options. What did they do when they were praised? Did they embarrass the person who praised them? Did they look big headed? Did they find the right words or just smile? Ask them to think about how they would act if they could go back and do it again. Would they act differently? Would they say different words? Discuss the alternatives.

Activity sheet

Read through the scenarios with the children. Remind them that they give as well as accept praise. Ask them to read the scenarios and write down how they would act.

Taking pride   My name is..

Read through these scenarios and consider how to respond. Write alongside what you would say and do in these circumstances.

what happened	what you would say or do
Someone has praised you for your good work in class. They said you take pride in all your work and made you stand up and praised you publicly.	
All your class had to stand up in Assembly and your teacher made you go up to collect the sports cup for your class.	
You entered a competition in your local newspaper and you won a prize. You had to go to the newspaper offices to collect it.	
You did some maths homework really quickly and got most of it wrong. Your teacher said, 'This is dreadful. I hope you feel proud of yourself!'	
You are top of your class in the recent test. Your friends are dismissive of this and accuse you of being big headed because you always do well.	
Your Dad runs a five a side football team at the local sports centre. You are always in the team and friends say this is just because your Dad runs it.	
Your little sister goes to ballet class and is really good at it. She practises a lot and sometimes has to do demonstrations.	

Turn over the paper.

When did you last praise someone? Write down what you said and did?

Celebrate

Talk about celebrations. Ask the children to think about celebrations; the kinds of things that they celebrate in their home and how they do it. Ask them to think about small celebrations and large celebrations. Write two headings on the board: small celebrations, large celebrations. Ask the children to finish the following sentence and consider whether it goes in the small or large celebrations list. List keywords they say.

'To celebrate in my family, we…'

Read through the lists; ask children to comment on both large and small celebrations.

To celebrate, we…

have a party
go out for a meal
tell our grandparents
give three cheers
buy presents
play games
say 'well done you'
send cards
clap people.

Birthday celebrations

Ask the children to think about how their family celebrate birthdays. Ask each child to write a report on the last birthday celebration in their family. Ask them to include words to describe how the birthday person felt and how other people in the family felt.

Achievement celebrations

Ask each child to think about how their family feels when the child has done something that needs celebrating. Can they tell the group of some of their achievements that the family celebrated? Were they achievements at home, at school or out of school? Ask them to say how they themselves felt when their family celebrated their achievement.

School achievements

Ask the children to close their eyes and think of their personal achievements at school. Without saying what these achievements were, ask children to say how they felt when some achievement of theirs, individually or as part of a team, was celebrated.

Talk about how your school celebrates achievement. Ask the children to list the ways you praise and celebrate what they do well within your classroom. Discuss the ways that your school, as a whole, celebrates achievement.

Moving on

Talk to the children about the time when they will be moving on to their next school. Help them to see it as a 'rite of passage', a celebration of the completion of their primary school years. Ask the children to write down a list of the things they have achieved in the primary school; not only in school work but also in their growth and personal development. Ask them to make sure to include things they are proud of achieving. Ask them to write about how they feel about moving on. Discuss their fears and worries and help them to understand that these are the same for every child who moves on.

Activity sheet

Ask the children to be realistic as they complete this. Explain that it could help your school to change the present celebrations and include new ones.

Celebrate   My name is...

Think of new ways to celebrate success at your school. Write three ideas of how you would like your teacher to celebrate with you in your classroom.

things we could celebrate in the classroom	how we could do it.
1.	
2.	
3.	

Write three ideas of how you would like to celebrate at school at dinner time.

things we could celebrate at dinner time	how we could do it
1.	
2.	
3.	

Turn over the paper.

Write down one good way your whole school celebrates at present. Write about the last time that happened and how you felt. Now think of two new ways for your whole school to celebrate. Describe how it could work.

Section 5　Five further lessons and activity sheets

The following topics with activity sheets should be used as part of the normal PSHE programme in school.

These lessons also aim to help to increase confidence. Explain to the children that when people feel confident they have high self-esteem. They feel ready and able to tackle new work and overcome obstacles.

topics	5–7 year olds	8–9 year olds	10–11 year olds
doing well	I am good at getting better	growing well learning well	working well working better
friendships	being a good friend what do I look for?	working with friends family friends	grown-up friends role models
joining in	I join in with friends I let others join in	working together playing together	including being welcomed
making choices	doing the right thing good persuasion	good choices difficult choices	healthy choices moral choices
feeling confident	co-operating in someone's shoes	assertiveness self belief	strengths control

We are all feeling good about coming to school

I am good at

Circle Time
Ask the children to think of something that they enjoy doing and to finish the sentence: 'I enjoy...'

Ask the children to think of something that they are really good at and to finish the sentence: 'I am really good at...'

Ask the children whether these are the same things. Talk about whether they think they:

- are good at something because they enjoy doing it
- enjoy doing something because they are good at it.

Draw a picture
Ask the children to draw a picture of something they are really good at doing and to write underneath the picture if they enjoy doing this.

How did you get good at it?
Talk with the children about how they became good at doing this thing:

- how did they learn to do it
- did someone help
- did they have to practise a lot
- was it easy or difficult to learn to do this
- did someone teach them?

Ask the children to work in pairs and each to choose one thing they are good at. Ask them to write down what this thing is and to write 'learning tips' on how they became good at doing it. Ask them to share their work with another pair before sharing it with the whole class. Make a list of all the 'learning tips' on the board. Then ask each child to choose one tip and to write it in a large speech bubble. Make a display using the children's drawings from 'Draw a picture' and these speech bubbles. Add an appropriate title and some questions and comments about the children's work. Share this display with other classes and teachers. Invite parents to look at the work and celebrate the many things that the children are good at.

Activity sheet
Explain how to do the activity sheet; about finishing the two sentences and that it is about doing something they are good at doing at school, not outside school.

I am good at

My name is.............................

Finish the sentences and draw a picture.

At school I am good at ....

....

....

At school
I enjoy doing

....

....

....

because............................

....

....

....

Turn over the paper.

Write about something else you enjoy doing at school. Are you good at doing this?

Doing well 5–7 year olds

Getting better

Circle Time

Ask the children to close their eyes and think of something they would like to be able to do better. Perhaps some skill they want to learn or some new work at school that they are learning; something realistic, not fantasy! Ask them to open their eyes and complete the sentence: 'I want to learn to .... better.' Jot down what the children say. Look at your list and ask the children to circle their responses in coloured sets; such as 'sport', 'classwork', 'creative activities' 'music'. Count how many are in each set. You could display this data in a chart or list with the message that these are things that the children are going to get better at.

I am going to get better at reading. I practise every day.

Remind the children that in the last lesson you talked about what you have to do to get better at doing things. Ask each child to draw a picture of themselves learning to get better at doing one of the things on the list and to write about what they have to do to get better at doing it.

Ask the children if they can think of any little steps they can take that will help them to get better at learning a new skill. For example in learning to read we use easy books to get started and practise frequently and in football we practise different ball skills alongside learning the rules of the game.

Don't be disheartened

Talk with the children about learning a new skill and making mistakes and getting it wrong. Explain that it is normal to do this but we mustn't be put off by making mistakes when we are learning. Ask the children to think back to when they were a baby learning to walk. It didn't happen overnight. Babies keep falling down and need to hold on to things before they walk properly. Ask the children to think back to learning a skill a year ago. Ask volunteers to tell the class about how they made mistakes and didn't get on well when they first started. Jot down these experiences and at the end remind children that these mistakes are part of learning new things and that they must remember this when they start something new. Ask the children to write about a young child learning to feed himself with a spoon.

Activity sheet

Explain that this is about getting better at doing something at home, **not** at school. It could be something to help at home, a sport, cooking or something outdoors, perhaps in the garden or on a sports field. They are to draw how they felt in the three boxes.

Getting better

My name is...........................

I am getting better at ....

I find it is ....(hard, easy)

....helps me.

1. When I started this I felt...................................

2. Now I am getting better I feel...................................

3. When I can do it, I will feel...................................

1. When I started I felt like this.	2. I'm getting better and I feel like this.	3. When I can do it I will feel like this.

Turn over the paper.

Draw yourself doing something out of school that you can now do well. Write what this is and how you feel now that you are better at doing this.

Growing well

Ask the chidren to think about how they have grown and changed since they became school children. Ask them to remember the first time they ever came to your school and how they felt then. Ask them to finish the sentence: 'When I first came to this school, I felt…'

Ask them to think of how they feel now that they have been in your school for some time. Ask them to tell you words to describe how they feel now. Make a list of these words alongside the first list. Talk about how confident and settled your children now feel. Ask them to tell you how this came about.

> **I felt…**
>
> happy
> excited, with friends,
> grown-up,
> good about it, scared,
> worried,
> unhappy, sad,
> no good, small,
> useless, inferior,
> overshadowed,
> nervous, anxious.
> timid.

How I feel now

Ask the children to reflect on the feelings in the first list and how they compare with how they now feel. Ask them to write about their feelings then and now as a comic strip, illustrating their writing with a sentence or phrase about each cartoon picture.

Design a poster

Talk to the children about the other changes in their bodies; they will be taller, heavier, with different teeth. Ask volunteers to tell you how they know they are growing; for example, their clothes won't fit, they will be able to reach things high up, they will eat more food. Ask them to work in small groups and to design a poster with pictures and writing about all the things that children need to have and to do, in order to grow well. Ask them to organise this task and decide who will do what. Give them a time limit for a finished poster for each group. Praise the children for their combined work and display the posters.

Thank you parents

Ask the children to think of all the things that their parents and carers have done in order for them to grow up well; for example, feeding them well, buying them clothes, teaching them to talk and walk, reading them stories. Ask each child to write a letter to their parents or carers in which they thank them for all they have done to help them to grow into confident and happy children.

Activity sheet

This is about the stages of their development. They draw themselves at the ages written in the first column and write in the other boxes.

Growing well

My name is...

a picture of me when I was...	how I looked	how I felt
2		
4		
6		
8		

Turn over the page.

Write what is good about being your present age. How do you feel?

Learning well

Ask the children to think what the phrase 'doing well' means. Ask volunteers to tell you times when people have used that phrase; not always about school work. Jot down what they say and talk about each one. Read through their contributions and ask them to draw a picture of someone doing well and to write what the person was doing well at.

My dad is doing well in hospital. He has been ill and it means that his body is getting better.

Ask the children to think about how they are growing and changing and whether they are all doing well at becoming the sort of person they want to be. Ask them to think of the qualities they want when they are grown up and the personality they want to have. Will this be a confident person? Will this be a shy and retiring person?

Work in pairs

Ask them to work in pairs and write a list of the qualities they would like to have when they are grown up, qualities that would help them to become the kind of person they want to be. Ask the pair to share this work with another pair and refine their list. Come together as a class and amalgamate the lists to give a profile of the kind of people the children in your class aspire to be when they are grown up.

What are you doing well at learning?

Ask the children to think of all the things they are learning to do. Ask volunteers to say what things they are getting better at learning. As well as listing school work accomplishments ask them to think about things they do out of school.

What qualities do you need to learn well?

Talk to the children about the personal qualities they need to be able to learn well. Ask them to finish the sentence: 'To learn well, we need to…' Jot down what they say and read through the list. Have they included qualities such as thinking about the task, not being easily distracted, persevering, concentrating organising time and resources? Help them to see that if they develop these qualities they will become efficient learners and be able to use these skills to learn all kinds of things as they grow up. Having good learning skills will help them to feel confident and able to tackle new work with enthusiasm.

Activity sheet

This is an opportunity for the children to assess their skills and to grade them into what they do well at, what they need to get better at and what they need to start learning to do. It could be enlightening for parents if the children take this home.

Learning well

My name is...........................

These are the skills we need so to learn well.

Draw ☐ to show the skills you already have
Draw ☺ to show the skills you are practising now
Draw ☹ to show the skills that you need to start learning.

Skills	☐☺☹
being able to read and understand instructions	
working well with a group	
working well in pairs	
working well individually	
organising myself	
selecting resources, finding the right ones	
organising time and not wasting it	
concentrating on what I'm doing	
not getting easily distracted	
having a positive attitude	
feeling confident, knowing I will do it well	

Turn over the paper.

Think about when you did some really good work in school. Write what this work was and the skills you had to use so that this was the best work you have ever done.

Working well

Talk to the children about how they set about new tasks and how they decide what they need to have and to do in order to set about new work. Ask volunteers to tell the class what they need in order to work well. Jot down what they say. Have they included such things as a good attitude, enthusiasm, drive and keenness. Talk about the need for people to have these attitudes if they want to do well.

Haiku

Ask the children to work in pairs and to write a haiku about what you need in order to work well and succeed. A haiku does not have to rhyme, has three lines with five syllables in the first line, seven in the second line and five in the third. Ask the class to come together and read out their haikus. Display the most apt and original.

> **Haiku**
>
> To work well you need,
> skill and enthusiasm,
> and the will to work.
>
> To work well is fine,
> be positive and think hard,
> you need drive and zeal.

Discuss

Ask the children to think about attitudes to working hard. Some people will always have a go and others seem to give up before they start. Ask them to think of the kind of people who would say the following:

- 'It's no good making a lot of effort I know it's going to go wrong.'
- 'I'm not sure how to do this, but I'll do the best I can.'
- 'I can't really be bothered with this. I'll just do the minimum.'
- 'This is really difficult, I'm going to need to find someone to help me.'
- 'Well this is hard, I'll look it up on the internet first.'

Ask them to decide which of these people have a positive attitude and which a negative one. Ask them to think which stand the best chance of getting it right and doing well.

Positive slogans

Ask the chidren to work in pairs and to write some slogans that might help people to think more positively about their attitude to work. After jotting down three or four slogans ask them to choose the best one to write up neatly in an eye catching way. Display these around the classroom. Make sure that the children read these occasionally to alert themselves to working in a positive way. Remind them that having a positive attitude to work makes success more possible and will give them confidence and self-esteem.

Activity sheet

This asks the children to think about different children's attitudes to school work. Can they think of some good advice to give them?

Working well

My name is..............................

Ask the children to think of their attitude to work. Ask them to write whether they think this is a person with a good work attitude in the second column and write yes, no or sometimes in the last column.

Work attitudes	Is this a person with a good work attitude?	Are you like this?
1. I'm always ready to work my socks off.		
2. I stay comfortable with my work and don't extend myself.		
3. I don't worry if people criticise me for working too hard.		
4. I feel embarrassed when people praise me; I usually say that it was easy and that anyone could have done it.		
5. I don't let other children persuade me to waste time at school or skip homework.		
6. I always like to go with the flow even if I know underneath that it's not exactly the right thing to do.		
7. I feel pleased when people praise my work and I can accept praise gracefully.		
8. I don't like admitting mistakes, I hope things will work out OK.		
9. I hate it when things go wrong. I try to put the blame on something or someone else.		

Turn over the paper.

Write down the numbers which show positive attitudes. Write some advice for each of the people with negative attitudes.

Working better

Talk to the children about working to their maximum as opposed to putting in the minimum effort. Ask them what the results will be in each case. Is it possible to do really well if people put in the minimum effort? Is it possible to fail if you do the maximum? Ask the children why they think that some people work hard and always do their best and some people can't be bothered.

Success can follow success

We know that if we succeed at something we are happy at moving on and doing more of that kind of thing. Ask the children to give you examples of some of the things that they have been successful at and which have led them to do more and better things. Ask each child to write about one success they have had recently that has made them want to do more of that kind of thing.

What about failure?

It can be hard to recognise that mistakes happen but we do all make mistakes. Tell the children of one mistake you have recently made and how it made you feel. Did it make you feel:

- you want to stop doing that activity
- you never want to try anything like that again
- you want to think of it as a learning experience
- you see where you've gone wrong and want to have another go?

Ask the children to share their failures with you and to say whether it made them give up or made them stronger.

Debate

Ask the children to think whether the people who said the following were positive learners or people with low self-esteem:

Failure just means you can't do it, so you may as well give up.

Failure means you made a mistake; learn from that and have another go.

You have to accentuate the positive and eliminate the negative.

Proverbs

There is a saying 'He who never makes a mistake never makes anything.' Ask the children to work in pairs and write some modern proverbs or sayings on this theme.

Activity sheet

Ask the children to write down the advice they would give to these letter writers.

Working better

My name is..............................

Some children in Apollo School are having a hard time of it at school. They keep failing and have written to Jaz in a children's magazine for help. Write replies to help these children.

Children's letters	Your replies to help them to work better
Dear Jaz, I just hate maths. I can't do it and am always getting it wrong. I just want to give up maths altogether but my teacher keeps shouting at me and telling me to try harder. I can't try any harder than I am doing. I can't sleep at night because of this. What should I do? Mary	
Dear Jaz, I'm really struggling with my reading. I can't remember the words and even at home my Mum gets mad at me. Sometimes I wish I just had easier books to read but my teacher says I have to read the book she gives me. The letters don't seem to make sense and I just don't know what to do. Zed	
Dear Jaz, All my mates love playing football but I can't get the hang of it. I kick at the ball and sometimes it doesn't seem to move at all and other times it goes in the wrong direction. My Dad wants to get me some coaching but I am afraid I won't be able to do it even then. What shall I do? Harry	

Turn over the paper.

Think of something that you find difficult and make mistakes in. Write down what this is and some good advice that you can give yourself so that you will keep trying and not give up.

Being a good friend

Drawing activity

Talk about friends and friendship. Ask the children to think of all the people who are special to them. These people could be children, grown-ups at home or grown-ups at school. Ask them to draw one of these people, write their own name and write underneath, 'This is my friend called...'

smile at people
make them smile
do things for them
help them
play with them
lend them things
think about them
invite them home
let them choose
not be bossy

Playing with friends

Ask the children to think of the friends they have at school. Perhaps they are the ones in their working group or perhaps they are in other groups or classes. Remind them that friends are really special people and that they are good to us and treat us fairly. They think of how we are feeling and make sure they are kind and friendly to us. Ask them to finish the sentence: 'A good friend is one who...'

Circle Time activity

Ask the children to finish the sentence, 'I show I am a good friend when I...' Jot down any interesting responses from the children. When everyone has had a chance to respond, read through your jotted list and talk about each one.

How do I feel?

Ask the children to think about how they feel when they are with their friends. Ask them to give you words to say how they feel and make a list of these feeling good words. Read through your list with the children and use it to make a list to display in the classroom so that children can use these words in their writing.

What have I done today to be a good friend?

Ask the children to close their eyes and think about being a good friend to someone. It could be a child or a grown up person. It could be someone in their family, in their neighbourhood or at school. Ask them to focus on something they have done today that shows they were a good friend to one of these people. Ask them to finish the sentence: 'Today I was a good friend to ... when...'

Activity sheet

Read through the activity sheet with the children and talk about any difficult words. Ask them to think about friends and what the activity sheet wants them to do. On the other side they have to draw themselves being a good friend.

Being a good friend   My name is.........................

wordbox

kind
happy
funny
share
smile
help
feel
good

It is <u>easy/not easy</u> to be a good friend because

....

....

These are the things I can do to be a good friend.

I can...

I can...

I can...

This is how I feel when I am being a good friend.

I feel...

and...

If my friends feel sad, this is what I do.

I...

I...

Turn over the paper.

Draw yourself being a good friend and write what you are doing.
Write how it makes you feel when you are being a good friend.

What do I look for?

Talk to the children about choosing new friends. What kinds of people do they like to be friends with? Do they like people who are bossy or who let them always choose? Talk about going to a new place where they have no friends and don't know anyone. Ask them to draw a picture of them in this new place and to write down the things that they will be looking for in making a new friend. Tell the children that you will read out what they have written so that you can share it with everyone, but that you won't say who wrote it.

Write these headings on the board; looks like, has, what he does, what he says. Collect the children's papers together and go through them reading out just the relevant things that the children say. Ask them to think whether these things are about what the new friend looks like, about what he has, about what he does or about what he says and ask a member of the class to put a figure one under the heading that best describes what each child has written. Talk about what their papers indicate that they are looking for in a new friend and ask the children whether these are the right things to look for.

Talk about the qualities that a good friend should have, such as loyalty, cheerfulness, ability to share, liking the same things.

When we're with our friends…

Ask the children to think about how they act towards their friends; do they play well together, listen to them, take turns, let others join in, be fair?

Make a friends poster

Ask the children to help you to make a poster to display in the classroom.

Ask them to:

- draw a picture of a child that fills a piece of A4 paper
- cut it out
- write some words that tell what this person is like, for example, their name, what they like to do, where they like to go
- draw a speech bubble around the words and cut it out.

Ask them to place their person and speech bubble on an A1 paper with lots of others so that they fill the paper. Display them all or vote on the best one to display in your classroom.

Activity sheet

Explain the activity sheet to the children; make sure they understand what they have to do.

What do I look for?　　　　　My name is..........................

| This is me looking for a new friend. | **wordbox**

 cheerful <br> happy <br> kind <br> friendly <br> football <br> games <br> play <br> park <br> picnic |

I am looking for a new friend
who is ....

and...........................

and...........................

They will like to..

....

Turn over the paper.

Draw this new friend that you are looking for. Write about them and how you will feel when you are with your new friend.

Working with friends

Pros and Cons

Ask the children whether they think it is good to work with their friends at school. What are the advantages of working in a group and what are the disadvantages? Ask the children to work in pairs and to write down a list of advantages. Share these with another pair and make one list. Share these with another four and make one list. Come together as a class and amalgamate the lists.

> **Pros**
>
> you can help each other
> it's more fun
> people give more ideas
> do the bits you're good at
> share the hard bits.

Now ask the children to do the same activity with the disadvantages. Look at the two sets of words. Do the pros outweigh the cons? Do they think that some children might coast along if they work in a group? Do they have to have a leader? Do some people get overlooked? Does everybody work or just some people?

How do you do it?

Ask the children to think of the last time they worked with a friend. Ask them to think of how they divided the work. Did they work side by side; did they:

- make a plan before they started
- each choose a part of the work
- share resources or each get their own
- share the work or did one do the writing while the other drew the pictures
- use each other's talents to best advantage?

Ask the children to write a report of how they did this last piece of shared work.

When can't you work with friends?

Ask the children to think about how they feel when they work on their own. What kinds of work have to be done alone? Do some of the children prefer to work alone? Does working alone make them want to talk to others while they are doing it? Ask them to finish one of these sentences: 'I prefer to work with friends because…' 'I prefer to work on my own because…' Ask the children to vote on whether they prefer to work alone, in pairs or in a group. Record these numbers. At the end of the term ask them to vote on the same issue. Have the numbers changed?

Activity sheet

The children have to work on their own to say whether they agree or not with the statements. When all have finished, ask them to work in pairs and compare their responses. Ask them, 'Does working with friends makes you feel more confident?'

Working with friends   My name is.....................................

Think about these statements and write whether you agree with them.

statement	agree don't agree
I like working with my best friend.	
I don't like working with other children, only my friends.	
I like working with all the children in my class.	
I like working with people who help me.	
I like working with people I can help.	
I like them to do the hard bits.	
I like to do the difficult bits.	
I get angry when we don't share work equally.	
I like to direct operations and be the boss.	
I like to work quietly without talking much.	
I like to talk a lot while I work.	
I like to work in a big group.	
I like to work in pairs with one other person.	
I have worked with every child in the class.	
I like to work in pairs with any child of the opposite gender.	
I don't like to work in a mixed gender group.	
I always work with the same person when we do paired work.	
I have only worked with a few children in this class.	
I really prefer to work on my own.	

Turn over the paper.

Write a letter to a pen friend about working with friends. Tell your pen friend whether you enjoyed this and what is good and not so good about working with friends.

Family friends

Talk with the children about friends that they have within their family. These may be near relations or distant ones. Do they think of siblings as friends or are siblings different from friends? When we say 'family friends' in this instance we mean people within the family who are also friends, not friends of the family.

Draw and write

Ask the children to draw their best friend in their family.

Ask them to draw this person and write about:

- who this person is
- how they are friendly together
- the kinds of things do they do together.
- whether this friend older or younger.

My family friend

This is Tom. He is my older brother. He plays with me and helps me to learn to do things. I love Tom. Harry

Who makes you feel good?

Talk to the children about other family friends.
Ask them to think about those who make them feel good about themselves. What kinds of things do these 'family friends' do to help them feel good about themselves, for example, play with them, praise them, help them to make or do things. Ask the children to complete the sentence: 'My family friend is. … and they make me feel good about myself when …'

Making them feel good

Talk about the kinds of things people can do to help 'family friends' feel good about themselves. Do young ones care for older ones? Do older ones care for younger ones? How do they feel when they are with very old family friends?

Family gatherings

Does their family have 'get togethers' when all the generations get together for a party or celebration? Talk about these kinds of gatherings, they may be once a year occasions, holidays, weddings, meeting new baby celebrations or religious parties. How do the children feel when they are in such a gathering? Do they have family friends of their own age that they play with? Ask the children to write about the last occasion when their family got together and had a celebration.

Discuss

1. Family parties are a nuisance, people just talk together and ignore me.
2. Family parties are wonderful times when we all get together and have fun.

Activity sheet

They have to draw many of their family friends; write names underneath. Then they choose three of these and write about the kinds of things they do together.

Family friends

My name is..

Draw lots of your family friends and write their names underneath.

One of my family friends is............................. This is what we do together.

Another family friend is.................................... This is what we do.

A third family friend is..................................... This is what we do.

Turn over the paper.

Choose a family friend who is younger than you. What kinds of things do you do together that make this friend feel good?

Grown-up friends

Talk with the children about their grown-up friends. These may be older members of their family or older people that they know and are friendly with. They may be friends from a different age school, people who live near or parents of their friends. Discuss the kinds of things that grown-up friends do that can help young people to feel good about themselves.

> ### Grown-up friends can...
>
> discuss things with us
> show us how to do things
> talk about world affairs
> talk about olden days
> help with projects
> teach us things
> tell their story
> share their ideas
> help us with learning.

Ask the children to think of one such friend and what this grown-up friend can give, in terms of support, to the friendship.

Grown-up friends' skills

Ask the children to think of any of the grown-up friends they know who have special skills or hobbies, such as musical, artistic or sporting skills. Ask whether these friends share their skills with them and whether this helps children in your class to feel good about themselves. Ask volunteers to tell the class.

Write a story

Ask the children to write a story about a child with low esteem but who has a really good grown-up friend. In the story, write how this friend helps the child to feel good about him/herself and become more self assured.

A disabled grown-up

Ask the children to think of some of the disabled grown-ups in the news; those who have used their disability as a challenge and have overcome many of their apparent limitations. Ask the children to work in pairs to research one disabled person and find out what this person can do and how they help themselves and, perhaps others, in spite of their disability. What kind of good things does this disabled person do? Could they be said to be an inspiration to people who are able bodied? Would they make a good friend?

A disabled grown-up friend

Ask the children to imagine a grown-up friend who is disabled in a wheelchair. Ask them to work in pairs and write a short list of the things they can do to help this disabled person. Come together as a class and discuss these options. Ask the children to think carefully about whether the disabled friend will be happy to receive this help or whether s/he would feel more accepted without it. What can the disabled friend give to the friendship?

Activity sheet

Ask the children to think about the kinds of friendships that could develop with the people in the pictures. Would they like to have friends such as these? Would the friendship be one-sided? How would each benefit?

Grown-up friends

My name is..

Write at the side of each picture why you would or would not like this person to be your friend.

A female model		sportsperson	
doctor		teacher	
racing car driver		eye specialist	
astronaut		male cleaner	
someone with a disability		police officer	

Turn over the paper.

Write about one of your own grown-up friends. How did the friendship come about? What are the mutual benefits of this friendship? Does the friend give you confidence and enhance your self-esteem?

Role models

Ask the children to think about people who are role models to young people of their ages. What kinds of people are these? Make a list. Are they always good role models? Do they live a lifestyle that your class would like to emulate? Are they real people or characters from TV, books or films?

pop stars
musicians
footballers
tennis players
TV stars
reality TV stars
people with power
sports coaches
teachers

Why would you like to be like them?

Ask the children to think of the kinds of skills and qualities these people have, that they themselves would like to have. What kinds of things make people into role models; their job, their popularity, their success, celebrity status, their lifestyle, their wealth? Ask them to write if and why they would like to be similar to these people.

Your role model

Ask the children to draw a picture of their own personal role model. Ask them to write about this person and say why they would like to be like him or her. Ask them to consider whether they have this person as a role model because of the person's lifestyle, wealth or because of the kind of person they are.

Being a role model

Ask the children to work in pairs and to discuss the responsibilities of people who are well known and are often role models to young and impressionable people like themselves. How should these role models behave? Do they have a responsibility to the young people who think of them as role models? Ask the children to jot down some ideas so they don't forget what they have been discussing before joining up with another pair to refine their jottings.

Come together as a class and, using ideas from the children's discussions write out a list of responsibilities of people who are role models.

Bad role models

Ask the children to think of some of the poor characteristics and personalities of well known people who might aspire to be role models. How do they think that young children will feel if their stars exhibit poor behaviour and disgrace their profession? Ask them to tell you what they would like to say to people such as these.

Activity sheet

This is about the personal qualities of people who are role models for children of different ages. Ask your children to ignore fame and fortune and concentrate on what the people are really like and what they do.

Role models

My name is.....................................

Ask the children to describe and draw ideal role models for children of different ages. Ask them to think of the personal characteristics of the person regardless of their celebrity status.

A good role model for a three year old would be someone who...

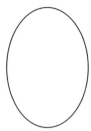

For a five year old a good role model...

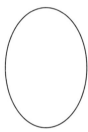

For a seven year old a good role model...

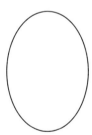

For a nine year old a good role model...

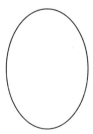

Turn over the paper.

Think of yourself as a role model for a seven year old in your school. How would it make you feel to be a role model to someone? Would it give you confidence and enhance your self-esteem? Write how you would feel and the qualities that you would like this seven year old to absorb from your personality and friendship.

I join in with friends

Circle Time

Talk to the children about playing alone and playing together. Ask the children to put up a thumb if they like to play alone. Count how many thumbs are up and note this.

Ask them to touch their noses if they like to play together with friends and make a note of how many. Are you, the teacher, surprised at this number?

Ask volunteers to finish the sentence: 'I like to play alone…' Talk about why each child likes to play alone and whether it is because what they are doing is a solo activity.

Ask volunteers to finish the sentence: 'I like to play with others when/because…' Talk about their reasons.

Draw pictures

Ask the children to draw two pictures; one of them playing alone and one playing with one or more friends. Ask them to write about what they are doing in their pictures and how they are feeling.

Joining in

Ask the children to think about how they feel when they see children playing a game and they want to join in. Ask the children to say what they do and to finish the sentence: 'When I want to join in a game, I…' Talk about what they say. Are these good things to do? Could they do it better?

I feel confident

Ask the children to reflect on what they said in the previous activity. Do they feel confident about asking to join in a game? Ask how many would feel OK about asking to play. Ask how many would find it difficult to ask to join in. Talk about feeling confident and able to ask to join in. What kinds of words would be good to use? What tone of voice? What kind of body language? How would they feel if they were allowed in the game? How would they feel if they were not allowed to play?

> **I would…**
>
> ask politely
> say please
> cheer them on
> show I wanted to play
> be prepared to wait
> encourage the others
> feel bad if I couldn't
> feel OK if I couldn't
> find another game
> play with someone else.

Activity sheet

Explain that the activity sheet is about playing with friends and joining in. Make sure the children understand what they have to write and draw. Allow children to take these papers home to share with their family.

I join in with friends   My name is...........................

One game I play with friends is.....................

....

When I play this game with friends, I feel.........

....

This is a picture of me playing with.....................	Write what you are playing and where you are.

Turn over the paper.

Draw some friends playing a game outdoors. Draw you going to join in. Write how you feel.

I let others join in

Circle Time

Talk to the children about playing games with friends and others wanting to join in. Explain that it is not fair to exclude children from their games and that everyone has a right to join in. Talk about times when it is easy to let others join in and ask the children to finish the sentence: 'It is easy to let others join in a game when…' Make a list of these times

> **It's easy to let others in when...**
>
> it's a game for lots
> there's room
> you want more players
> it's football
> they're friends.

Ask volunteers to tell you of rare times when it's not possible to let other children join in their games; make a list of these. It may include, when teams are even, when it's a game for two or four and you've got that number, when the game's nearly over, when you'd need more apparatus.

Remind the children that even if there is a very good reason not to allow others in a game it is important to explain why and to do this with acceptable words and body language.

How do you feel?

Ask the children how they feel when they let others into a game. Does it make them feel good that the person wants to join them? Does it make them feel good when they are able to make someone else feel good? Ask them to finish the sentence: 'When I let someone in a game it makes me feel…' Make a list of these good feelings.

Tell a story

Jacob always seemed to want to play on his own. He never joined in group games. One day he saw some children from his class having a really happy time playing with a ball in the school playground and he wandered near to watch. He really did want to join in but didn't feel he could ask. May saw him watching and said 'Do you want to join in?' Jacob's face suddenly broke into a huge smile as he shyly said 'Yes please.'

Ask the children to tell you how they think that Jacob felt and also how May felt. Can they remember inviting someone into their game? Can volunteers tell the group about it? Is it better to invite someone to join in than to wait for them to ask?

Activity sheet

Make sure the children know how to do the activity sheet. You could make a display of them, perhaps in a corridor so that other classes could share.

I let others join in　　　　　My name is...........................

I think it is good to let children join in because.....

wordbox
feel
good
sad
unhappy
better
game
more
people
share

....

....

Draw a picture of children playing a game with someone watching who has not joined in.

I think the watcher feels ....

I would say..

Turn over the paper.

Draw another picture of the same game with the watching child joining in. Write about the game and how everyone feels.

Working together

Ask the children to think of all the various cultures in your school. Ask volunteers to name these various cultures and write their names on the board. Talk with the children about the differing ways that people from these cultures live and ask if some of these ways make people more self confident or less self confident. Ask the children to work in pairs and jot down the things they would like to include in a questionnaire.

As a class, read through these ideas and discuss the best ones and discard any that could make people feel uncomfortable or upset.

> **we could ask about...**
>
> foods
> drinks
> music
> celebrations
> clothes
> language
> roles of men and women
> religion
> attitude to school

Questionnaire

Ask the children to work with a different partner, one of the opposite gender, and design a questionnaire that they could use to interview all children, whatever their culture, in your class or school. Ask children to put these in a safe place so that you can read through them before they are used. Make sure that the first question is asking about how the children feel about responding to this questionnaire and that none of the questions can cause offence.

Finding answers

Ask the children to work in their pairs and to visit others in the class or year group to find answers to the questionnaire. Come together as a class; ask the children to report on the experience of asking questions and discuss what they have discovered.

Hidden agenda

Explain what a hidden agenda is – something that you really would like to do or find out without asking direct questions. Ask your children to tell you whether they think that any of the children they interviewed:

- like working with children from other cultures
- prefer to work within their culture group
- feel good about working together in your school
- enjoy being with others from various cultures
- of whatever culture, feels that they are a valued part of the school community
- feel isolated or uncomfortable within your school community.

Ask the children what else they discovered about the feelings of people from all cultures joining in school life.

Activity sheet

Explain that this is about children from various cultures working together. They have to write down good, positive responses to the statements the children have made.

Working together   My name is...

These are negative comments from children who have been working together. What would you say to these children?

He won't let me do it for myself.	
He always thinks he knows best.	
I think he ought to do it my way.	
Those two always work together.	
I don't want to work with a boy.	
I don't want to work with a girl.	
I have to do all the work.	
He won't help me.	
I want to work with Jazza instead.	

These are positive comments from children who have been working together. What would you say to these children?

We really work well together don't we?	
We both like to work quietly.	
He helps me and I help him.	
It's really good working together.	
We often try new ideas together.	
Sometimes we do it my way and sometimes my partner's way.	
We have different skills so we work well together.	
I am more confident when we work together.	

Turn over the paper.

Write three good reasons for working in pairs with someone from a different culture. Write three good reasons for working in a mixed culture group of children. Write three good reasons for working in a mixed gender group.

Playing together

Ask the children to work in a group and jot down all the activities or games they know that they can play alone. Ask them to put these in lists of 'active games' 'creative games' 'other games', computer games'. Ask a spokesperson from one group to read out their list and then ask other groups to add to the lists. Are the children surprised at the number of alone games?

> **Alone games**
>
> cards, drawing and painting, running, patience game, solitaire, reading, making things, knitting, cooking, playing ball, skipping, writing stories, music, PC games.

Team games

Talk to the children about their team games, for example, the team games that they play in school and at home, the places where they play, how the games are organised, how teams are chosen and so on.

Ask the children to work alone and describe a team game that they play or would like to play. Following this you could ask the children to tell you the names of the games and how many of them like each one.

Rules

Talk about the rules for sports and games. Are the rules for team games clear and strict? Do the children ever cheat when playing as a team? Is it the game that is important or who wins?

Is it easy to cheat when playing alone? Are the children able to play to the rules or do they cheat when playing, for example, solitaire or patience? Is it the game that is important or completing or winning it?

Discuss

It is better to play a good game and lose than play a poor game and win.

After the discussion ask children to say whether this statement is true or false for them.

Grown-up teams

Ask the children if they follow any grown-up teams or sports and talk about these. Do you have a local football team? Do the children follow cricket, tennis or other sports? How many children are fans of any team? What do they do to be a fan?

Activity sheet

The children are asked to write about the games they like to play, either alone or with other children. The 'turn over' section asks about personal qualities not equipment.

Playing together

My name is...........................

A game I like to play alone is..

because...

A game I like to play with other children is.......................................

because ....

I do/don't like to play team games because...

A team game I do play is...

I like/don't like this game because...

A team game I like to watch is..

because...

Turn over the paper.

1. Write about what you need in order to play together well with other children.
2. Write about what you need to play a good team game with other children.
3. Write about what grown-ups need to have and to do to be in a team.

Including

Talk with the children about the importance of including other children in their work or play. Ask them to think about how it would feel to be left out of games or work. Ask volunteers to give you 'feelings' words and jot these down. Ask the children to think of any time when they have been left out. Ask them to tell the group about what this could have done to their self-esteem.

> **Excluded people feel...**
>
> sad, unhappy, rejected, unworthy, useless, overlooked, no good, ineffective, a waste of time, ignored, worthless, undeserving, not good enough.

What do people do?

Ask them to think about stories they have read, TV dramas or films when someone has been left out and tell you about:

- how the characters felt
- how they reacted
- what it did to their self-esteem
- how it affected other people
- whether they went on to commit anti-social acts.

Discuss these before the children do the following activity.

Write about it

Ask the children to choose one character from book or film and write about the outcome of that person not being included. Ask them to write what advice they would have given to the character and what they themselves would have done in those circumstances.

Discuss

Why do some people try to exclude others from their work or play?

As the children give reasons for exclusion, discuss each one. Have they included differences in age, gender, ability, race, culture, religion, ethnicity? Explain that this is discrimination. Discuss if there are ever good reasons for not letting people join in.

Have you ever done it?

Ask the children to spend a minute or two in silent reflection on whether they have ever excluded someone from work or play. Ask them to reflect on how that person may have felt and whether it made them do something rash or anti-social. Ask them to reflect on how it made them feel themselves, to deliberately exclude someone. Do they realise that this is a form of discrimination or bullying? Ask volunteers to share their thoughts.

Activity sheet

The children are asked to consider good reasons for including and not excluding others in their work and play and to describe a scenario where someone is about to be excluded before their intervention. It would be useful to discuss what the children write.

Including

My name is.............................

Ask the children to write down four good reasons for making sure they include other people when they are working.

1.

2.

3.

4.

Ask the children to write down four good reasons for making sure they include other people when they are playing.

1.

2.

3.

4.

Ask the children to write down two good reasons for never excluding people from joining in.

1.

2.

Turn over the paper.

Write a scenario in which someone tries to exclude someone from their team. Write what both characters do. Write what you would say to the person trying to exclude the character and then write a good ending to the scenario.

Joining in 10–11 year olds

Being welcomed

Ask the children to think of a time when they felt new and alone somewhere and someone made them feel welcome. Ask the children to think about their feelings when they realised that they could join in this new group and be included. Jot down the feelings words. Ask them to show by their faces and body language how they would feel.

> **Feeling welcome**
>
> great, wanted, included, with them, friendly, sociable, pleasant, companionable, in good company, sought after, chummy, comfortable, wicked.

Role play

Ask the children to work in groups of four or five with one of them being the new person and the others being the welcoming group. Ask them to mime how they would welcome this person into their group. No words! Ask the children to change over roles so that every person is the new member of the group. Come together as a class and discuss the feelings both of the new person and the welcoming group.

How can you do this?

Talk with the children about how you go about setting someone at their ease and including them in a class or closed group. What kinds of things would you say to them? Would you ask them lots of questions? Would you tell them about yourselves and what the group is doing? Would you help them to know how they could fit into the group? Jot down what the children say and discuss each one. Are they all effective? Could some be intrusive?

Open and closed questions

Discuss with the children the nature of open and closed questions. Explain that closed questions only have the answers 'yes' or 'no'. Ask them for examples of closed questions. Ask for examples of open questions. Which do they think would be more useful to use with new people coming into a group?

What would you say?

Ask the children to work in small groups and imagine that they are going to welcome a speaker to your school. This person is going to speak to the children about something important. What could a welcoming group say to this person as they greet them? Ask them to write down some sentences and questions that would be non-intrusive and welcoming. Ask a spokesperson from each group to read out what they have written and discuss each one.

Activity sheet

Children are asked to consider how to integrate a newcomers into their class.

Being welcomed   My name is.....................................

A new student is coming to your classroom. How do you think this student would be feeling?

I think the new student would be feeling…

What would you do and say to make this student feel welcome?

I would say…

I would say…

I would do…

I would do…

A new classroom assistant is coming to work in your classroom. This person has never worked in a school before. How do you think they are feeling?

I think they are feeling….

What would you say or do to make this person feel welcome in your classroom?

I would…

Turn over the paper.

Your teacher, whom you really like, is away sick. The headteacher brings in a temporary teacher whom you don't know. Write down how you think this teacher is feeling, how you are feeling and what you will do to help this teacher feel welcomed.

Making choices 5–7 year olds

Doing the right thing

Circle Time

Ask the children to think about the choices that they make every day. Do they always choose the correct thing to do? Do they sometimes wish they had chosen to do something different? Remind the children that we always feel good when we choose to do the right thing and usually feel bad when we choose to do the wrong thing. Ask volunteers to finish the sentence: 'I chose to do the right thing when I...'

> I chose to do the right thing when I picked up the paper I dropped.

Head or heart?

Ask the children to think of their feelings and how they feel when they make the wrong choice. Ask them where in their bodies they feel these feelings. Make a list of these places, such as, in your chest, your heart, your head. Explain to the children that they make choices to do things using their head or brain, which knows the correct thing to do, or using their heart, which knows what they really want to do. Sometimes your heart makes you want to make the wrong choice. Can any of the children tell the class of some poor choice they made using their heart when they knew in their head that it was the wrong thing to do?

Tell a story

Soria loved chocolate. She had a little every day after her evening meal. Her parents said it was a good time to eat chocolate and she would clean her teeth soon before going to bed. She knew where the chocolate was kept and she often felt that she would like to help herself to some during the day. One day she felt so unhappy and just knew that a piece of chocolate would cheer her up. When no one was in the kitchen, she went to the cupboard and took half a bar of chocolate and went up to her room and ate it. She ate it all. It tasted so good. It didn't cheer her up though; she began to feel rather bad instead.

Ask the children to tell you why Soria thought that chocolate would cheer her up. What made her take it? Why didn't it make her feel good? What could she do to make herself feel better about the bad choice she had made? Talk about making the wrong choice and feeling bad about it. Talk about making the right choice and feeling good about it. What other things could Soria have done to cheer herself up if she felt unhappy? What would they have done instead?

Activity sheet

The activity sheet relies on the children understanding the last activity. Explain that they have to write about the choice Soria made and a better choice she could have made.

Doing the right thing   My name is..............................

Soria made the wrong choice when she... She felt...	**wordbox** took ate chocolate upset unhappy bad worried

Draw Soria doing the right thing and not taking the chocolate. Write at the side how she would have felt then.

draw here	write here

Turn over the paper.

Draw a picture of you making the correct choice. What are you doing? How are you feeling?

Good persuasion

Explain to the children that sometimes people try to persuade us to do something we don't really want to do. Sometimes the persuasion is good and makes us do things that are right even if we don't want to do them, for example eat things that are good for us. Sometimes the persuasion is not good and people might want us to do something that we know is wrong. Explain that good persuasion makes us feel good about ourselves because we know we are pleasing people and doing the right thing. Bad persuasion is always wrong and we must resist this.

Tell a story

Bazil was usually a very happy boy. He loved to play football and had lots of friends. He wasn't very good at reading though and often forgot to take his book home to read to his parents; so his reading wasn't getting any better. His dad thought about this. 'Persuasion might help', said his mother, so his dad thought some more. Then he came up with an idea; 'If you bring your book home every night for a month and we read it together each night, I'll organise a treat for you.' Bazil didn't really like the idea, but the thought of a treat persuaded him. He remembered to take his book home; they read every night and in no time at all his reading had improved no end. When the end of the month came he chose to go to the pictures with his Mum and Dad. His teacher was pleased and wondered how he'd managed to improve so much. 'Dad persuaded me.' he said.

Ask the children if they thought this was good persuasion. Can any of them remember someone persuading them to do something that was good for them?

Write a postcard

Ask the children to write a postcard to Bazil congratulating him on his good reading. They can use the name of your school. Ask them to draw Bazil on the other side.

Congratulations on your good reading Bazil. You must feel really good about that. I am glad your dad persuaded you to practise so hard. Well done from Jonty	Bazil Brown Anytown school Anytown Hampshire	

Activity sheet

Read through the activity sheet with the children and explain that it is about themselves being persuaded to do something good.

Good persuasion   My name is..............................

I was persuaded to ....

....

When I had done it I felt ....

....

This is me being persuaded to do
something good for me.

Before I did it I felt......

....

Now I feel...

Turn over the paper.

Draw a picture of you persuading someone to do something good
for them. Write how you feel. Write how they feel when they've
done it.

Making choices 8–9 year olds

Good choices

Ask the children what kinds of choices they have to make at home. Do they decide what to wear? Do they decide what to eat? Ask them to finish the sentence: 'I can choose…' Jot down some of the interesting choices that they are allowed to make for themselves.

> **I can choose…**
>
> what to play
> what to read
> the fruit I like
> my favourite drink
> things to wear
> where to play
> who to ask to tea
> who to play with
> what to watch on TV.

Not my choice

Talk about choices that the children are not allowed to make for themselves, what these choices and why are they not allowed to make them. Is it because of safety or health?

Fair choices

Talk to the children about being fair when they choose to do things with friends. Do they always play fair? Could some of their choices be unkind or be difficult for other children to accept? Ask them to reflect on times when their choices have not been fair.

Read these scenarios and ask the children to tell you whether the choices were fair or not:

Kendy had told Josh that he would be going with him to the cinema on Saturday. On Saturday morning Charlie rang up and asked him if he would like to go to his house and have a barbecue. Kendy thought he could put Josh off and asked his brother to phone him to say he was ill and couldn't go to the cinema after all. Then he went to the barbecue.

Jan didn't want to go to the sleepover at Josie's even though she had accepted. She told Josie that her Mum wouldn't let her. Jan stayed at home and watched TV.

Zak had put the cakes on a plate but one of them had fallen on the floor. He picked it up and put it back on the plate. Then he took the cakes into the sitting room and offered them to his guests. He made sure he didn't take that cake!

Daisy wanted to give Mum a present for Mothers' Day. She had some money but she really wanted the money for herself. When she was walking to the shop she saw some daffodils outside a garden on the verge. She picked the flowers and took them home. They looked quite good when she wrapped them up and gave them to Mum.

Chris wanted to listen to Kim's new birthday CD but he knew she wouldn't let him. He sneaked it out of her room and went to Jake's house to play it. After playing there for a bit he went home and forgot the CD. Back at home, Kim was looking everywhere for it; Chris didn't know what to say so he didn't say anything.

Ask the children to suggest alternatives to make these scenarios fair.

Activity sheet

Explain that the children have to decide which are good and poor choices and why.

Good choices   My name is...............................

Think whether these are good or not good choices.

	Is this a good or bad choice? Why?
buying fruit that is past it's sell by date	
having a good breakfast before school	
telling a lie about something	
making sure you do your homework on time	
helping your parents at home	
throwing litter in the pond	
taking a dog for a walk without a lead	
eating four bars of chocolate at once	
not going to sleep at the right time	
not doing your homework	
not getting angry when you're told off	
listening to what your grown-ups say	

Turn over the paper.

Think of a time when you had to make a choice and you made the correct one.
Write about what the choice was and what you chose. What happened next?
What could have happened if you had made the wrong choice?

Making choices 8–9 year olds

Difficult choices

Ask the children to think about times they have had to make difficult choices, when they have had to do something they didn't want to do but they knew they had to, for example wanting to watch TV but knowing they have to do homework, or wanting to go out with friends but staying at home to look after a young sibling. Ask the children to give examples and discuss each one.

My sister broke her leg and I wanted to go and play football but I stayed at home to keep her company.

Write about it

Ask each child to think of a story, film or scene on TV where someone had to make a difficult choice. Ask them to write about it and illustrate their work. Ask them to write what would have happened if the character had made a different choice.

Jed's difficult choice

Read this scenario to the children and discuss the various options.

Jed was nine years old and was quite good at football. His teacher wanted him to join the local children's team which meant going every Saturday morning to a club about six miles away. Dad always spent Saturday morning taking Jed's older sister to gym club and Mum, who worked, always spent Saturday mornings shopping and doing housework. He knew there was no way he could get to the club without someone taking him. No one was free to take him. They would feel bad if he told them and he couldn't go. Should he tell them or just forget it?

What would you do?

Ask the children to work in pairs to discuss this scenario and to list the various options. Come together as a class and list what you think is the best thing to do.

You find out that one of your best friends has been taking sweets from the local shop. You know the shopkeeper, who is Asian and he is really good to the kids in the neighbourhood. You want to stop your friend from stealing but you don't want to lose her friendship. You don't want the shopkeeper to find out and think you are stealing too. You know the local police officer who lives near you but you don't really want to get your friend into trouble. You just want him to stop stealing. What can you do?

Role play

In groups of four, act out the various solutions to the above problem. Is it difficult to find the right words to do the right thing? Change roles. Discuss your feelings.

Activity sheet

Children are asked to suggest the best choice to make in a difficult situation.

Difficult choices   My name is.................................

Write down the various choices that you could make. Which would you choose and why?

Ross is in a wheelchair and gets angry when people try to help him. You are going on a school trip and you would like to help by staying near and helping Ross but you think that he will get annoyed. What can you do?	
Louise is having a birthday party and you have been invited. Your greatest friend Anna hasn't been invited because Louise doesn't like her. Louise would like to come between you and Anna and break up your friendship. Should you say anything to Anna? Should you go to the party or not?	
Jed has broken his arm and won't be able to be in the archery tournament. All his family were going to watch and you were going with them. Now they aren't going and you don't know whether to go to the competition or stay behind and keep Jed company.	
By accident, you spoiled a painting that a girl in your class has done. She is upset because the teacher had said it was a good painting. No one knows who did it. You haven't owned up because it will get you in trouble. You feel bad in yourself. What can you do?	

Turn over the paper.

Think of a time when you have had, or may have, to make a difficult choice. Write down the options and say which you will choose to do.

Healthy choices

Foods and drinks

Ask the children to think about the health choices they make. Are these always the correct choices or could some of them do harm or be dangerous? If they always chose to eat chocolate and nothing else, or always chose to drink fizzy drinks and drink nothing else they would not be very healthy. Ask the children to think of healthy choices; the foods and drinks that will help them to grow up healthily. Ask them to work in pairs to write a list of healthy foods and drinks. Come together as a group and talk about the choices on their lists. Are they all healthy ones? Remind them that making healthy choices helps you to look good and feel confident.

> **Foods and drinks**
>
> water, milk, cheese, low fat spreads, brown bread, carrots, broccoli, cabbage, pasta, lean meat, oily fish, beans, spinach, apples, bananas, grapes, oranges, plums.

Exercise is fun

Ask the children why they think it is good to take regular exercise and which parts of the body benefit from exercise. Talk about what can happen to our bodies if we don't exercise. Ask the children to tell you all the kinds of exercising that they do, for example, walking, running, games, swimming and so on. Talk about the fun element in exercise; for example, is it more fun running about playing football or walking on a walking machine in a gym?

Write about it

Ask the children to write a convincing argument to persuade people to do the exercise that they like best.

Sleep and rest

Ask the children to work out how many hours sleep they get each school night. Ask those who sleep for nine hours to stand in a certain place and do the same with ten hours, eight and so on until all the children are in a group. Ask the groups to count themselves and make a quick graph on the board to show the lengths of time that people in your class normally sleep. You can include yourself and the classroom assistant. Are the children surprised at these sleep times?

Find out

Ask the children to work in pairs to find out why it is important to get the right amount and the right kind of sleep, what happens when you sleep, what happens if you don't get enough sleep and to write a short report on sleep. Discuss what they find out and whether children in your class are making the right healthy choice with regard to sleep.

Cleanliness

Talk about keeping your body clean as a healthy choice. Debate the benefits of baths versus showers and deodorants versus washing.

Activity sheet

Children have to assess the lifestyles of people and suggest improvements.

Healthy choices

My name is............................

Being healthy or not is a choice we make. Decide whether these people are living a healthy lifestyle or not and why. What could they do better?

The post person, who walks with his bag of post every day, never eats fruit or veg and who sleeps a full eight hours each night.	
The teacher who drives to school and back and sits all evening, eating fruit, preparing work and marking books.	
The doctor who plays squash in his lunch hour twice a week, snatches a sandwich for lunch and gets hardly any sleep.	
The footballer who practises regularly so that he will be in trim for the matches, eats a good breakfast and healthy food every night.	
The busy mother who walks her children to school and spends the morning on home cooking and housework.	
Dad, who takes his children to school by car, drives all over the country visiting factories, and snacks 'on the hoof' all day.	
The grandfather who walks to the corner shop every morning for the paper after a good breakfast and has a nap after lunch.	
The school child who won't eat breakfast, plays on a play station after school until late, who snacks all evening and arrives at school looking tired and peaky.	

Turn over the paper.

Write an accurate description of your lifestyle and whether it is really healthy or not healthy enough. What are you doing that is healthy? What are you doing that is not so healthy? Choose one healthy choice that you can make to improve your lifestyle and make it healthier. Write down how you will make sure you make this one new choice.

Making choices 10–11 year olds

Moral choices
Bring into school several newspapers, local and national.

Discuss the meaning of the word 'moral'. Ask the children to give you synonyms for this word. Ask children to take each word in turn and suggest a sentence containing it.

Moral means...

ethical
good
right
honest
decent
proper
honourable
just
respectable
worthy

Immoral actions
Share out the newspapers between small groups of children and ask them to look through to find reports of people who have acted in immoral ways. Ask them to cut out or write a précis of these occurrences. Come together as a class and discuss each one. Ask the children to discuss why the person or people behaved in that way. Ask them to decide what the people could have done, what they should have done, what they could now to repair the damage and what they themselves would have done in that situation. If the person was punished, ask the children to consider whether they think the punishment was just or whether they can suggest a different one.

Moral actions
Again, share out the newspapers between different, and this time, mixed gender groups of children. Ask them to look for examples of people showing that they have good morals. Explain that there may not be so many of these as good actions are not as newsworthy as bad actions. Ask each group to select one good moral occurrence and to discuss this within their group. As a class talk about the moral actions of the person or people concerned. Did they put themselves in danger to do the right thing?

The courage of Mr Jones
Discuss this example, whether the person did the right thing, the outcome and other possible outcomes.

Mr Jones, a 25 year-old man was walking his dog when he saw four youths taunting a black youth, shouting out, swearing and calling him names. Mr Jones stopped, called out to the youths and remonstrated with them. One of them moved towards Mr Jones, but when his dog barked loudly the four youths fled. Mr Jones spoke to the black youth who thanked him. The police are searching for these four youths using the descriptions that Mr Jones was able to give.

Missing woman
Ask the children to comment on this report from the *Daily Star*... When Miss Smith's dog fell in the river, she jumped in after it to try to save it. She has not been seen since but the dog scrambled out of the river and is safe.

Activity sheet
In these moral dilemmas, children are asked to help others to make the correct choice.

Moral choices

My name is..........................

Ask the children to write down what they would say to help the person to make the correct moral choice.

James saw a woman drop her purse in the shopping mall. It was kicked to one side. It looked full of money and cards. No one else seemed to have seen it. He could easily pick it up and keep it. He could buy loads of games for his Wii.	
Sahira was jealous of Zara and hid her library book so that Zara would be in trouble. Jan saw what happened but she was friends with both girls and didn't know what to do. If she told on Sahira that would be letting down one friend. If she didn't tell, then Zara would be in trouble.	
Josh saw a little boy playing in the park. There didn't seem to be anyone with him and he looked lost and alone. Josh was on his way to his music lesson and was already late. He really didn't have time to spare for a lost kid.	
Zoë's friend Alice was overweight and trying to eat healthily but Zoë knew that Alice was secretly eating biscuits and cakes on the way home from school. She often ditched her healthy lunch and filled herself up with junk food. Zoë really wanted to help Alice but when she mentioned it Alice always accused her of nagging. Zoë knew she ought to do something about it; but what?	

Turn over the paper.

Reflect on some moral dilemmas you know about from films or TV. Choose one and think up a really good way for the character to act in a morally responsible way. Write it as a dialogue, using apostrophes. Alternatively write it as a comic strip with speech bubbles.

Co-operating

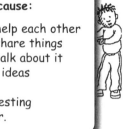

It's good to work in pairs because:

you can help each other
you can share things
you can talk about it
you have ideas
it's fun
it's interesting
it's easier.

Circle Time
Explain to the children that sometimes it's good to work alone, sometimes it's good to work with another child and sometimes it's good to work with a group of children. Ask them to think about whether they like to work with others. Ask volunteers to finish the sentence: 'I like to work with another child because...' Jot down what they say on the board. Read through their responses and talk about them. Explain that working with others can help you to feel confident.

Ask volunteers to finish the sentence: 'I like to work with a group because...'

Add these responses to the list on the board.

A shared task
Ask the children to work in pairs to measure their table. Call them A and B. Ask them to think of what they will need and collect these things. Ask A to measure how long it is first with a tape and B to write down the length. Ask B to measure how wide it is and A to record it. Ask them to continue measuring the table until they have at least six measurements, including height, length of leg, width of leg circumference of leg. Ask each pair to work with another pair working at a similar table and compare their measurements. Are they the same? Are they different? Come together as a group and talk about the task. Talk about whether it was better to work as a pair and then as a group rather than to work alone. Did they do the task better because they had two or four people sharing it?

Draw a picture
Ask the children, in the same fours to write about and make one shared picture of the shared task. Explain that they will have to talk about how to share this task before they do it and organise who does what. Ask each child to sign this work.

Alone or pairs
Ask the children to fold a paper in half and put a heading on each half; 'alone', 'pairs'. Ask them to jot down the names of three activities that are better done alone and three things that are better done pairs. Ask them to illustrate their work with small drawings showing the activities. Come together as a class and share this work.

Activity sheet
Read through the sheet with the children. Explain what they have to do.

Co-operating

My name is.......................... ..

I like to work alone when...

I like to work in a pair when...

I like to work in a group when...

wordbox
maths
reading
computer
painting
game
football
swimming
races.

Draw a picture of someone working in a group. Write at the side what the group are doing.

draw here	write here

Turn over the paper.

Draw yourself working in a large group. Write what you are doing and if you feel more confident or less confident when you work in a group.

In someone's shoes

I felt sad for Cinderella when her sisters were horrid to her.

Circle Time

Talk to the children about thinking of how other people are feeling. Remind them of a story you have recently told them, for example, *Cinderella*. Ask volunteers to tell the group how they felt when the main character did something wrong, difficult or sad. Did they share the feelings of the main character? Talk about another story you have told them about when things went wrong, for example, *Jack and the Beanstalk*. Did they put themselves into the shoes of the person when things went wrong? Explain that sharing these feelings is called empathy. It makes you feel confident if you can share feelings.

Tell a story

Edwin was a very kind boy who walked to school with his friend Sasha and her mum. Sasha's dog Gyp always went with them to school and had to be tied up outside the school gate as he wasn't allowed in the playground. It always made Edwin sad when he saw this. Gyp didn't like being tied up there and would whine a little. Edwin always waited until Sasha's mum went out of the playground and untied Gyp because Gyp would give a little jump to show he was pleased. One awful day Sasha and her mum didn't have Gyp with them. Edwin asked why there was no Gyp and Sasha started to cry and told him that Gyp had run into the road and got run over. Edwin was shocked. He put an arm around Sasha and said that he knew just how she felt.

Ask the children how they think that Sasha and Edwin were feeling. Edwin was trying to put himself into Sasha's shoes to feel what she was feeling. Ask them what kinds of things Edwin could do to try to make her feel better. How would this make him feel? Would Edwin feel confident if he could share Sasha's sad feelings?

In someone's shoes

Ask the children if they can think of someone else who put themselves into someone else's shoes and showed empathy. Ask volunteers to tell the class. Ask them then to try to finish the sentence: 'I put myself in …'s shoes when…'

Write a picture story

Ask the children to work in pairs to think up a story of someone showing empathy. Ask them to draw five or six pictures that will tell the story. Ask them to share writing just one sentence for each picture. Display some of these.

Activity sheet

Explain that they must finish the sentences and then draw pictures to tell the story.

In someone's shoes

My name is.........................

I put myself in someone's shoes when…

Our teacher put herself in someone else's shoes when…

Ken lost his cat and was sad.	I put myself in his shoes. I felt sad for him.	We looked everywhere.
I felt sad for the cat. I think it would be scared.	Then we found it.	I felt happy for Ken. I felt confident.

Turn over the paper.

Draw someone feeling sad. Write why they are sad. Write about feeling confident that you can feel their sadness and help them.

Assertiveness

Discuss

Assertive means always getting your own way.

Assertiveness means shouting others down.

Assertive means not being pushed about.

Assertive means having self confidence and high self-esteem and being able to explain yourself.

Assertive means

being self confident, having high self-esteem but not being pushy or aggressive.
I was assertive when I said I wanted to be included in the list.

Ask the children to write out their own definition of 'assertive' and to write a sentence using the word assertive or assertiveness. Ask the children to read out their definitions and discuss those sentences that showed a good understanding of the word.

Assertive or aggressive?

Talk about the difference between being assertive and being aggressive. Ask the children to give examples of each. Explain that confident people are usually assertive; they speak up and aren't easily put off and that they usually do this in a quiet but firm way. Aggressive people often resort to shouting and bullying tactics.

Role play

Ask the children to work in pairs and to practise being assertive in a polite and sensitive way. Give them some scenarios to enact, making sure that the pairs change roles. Scenarios could include:

- taking something they have bought back to the shop because it doesn't fit
- making an appointment at the dentist on a certain day at a certain time
- facing up to someone who is trying to persuade them to do something wrong.

Ask volunteers to show their role play to the class and discuss how effective the assertive person was.

Being assertive when necessary

Remind the children that it is not always necessary to show an assertive streak. It often makes life easier to 'go with the flow' unless the 'flow' is not good or can cause difficulties or problems. Is the assertive person always right? Can assertiveness prompt people to behave in a non-characteristic way sometimes? Explain that it is essential to get the balance right. Assertive enough not to be bullied or persuaded into doing something wrong and yet not so assertive that people don't want to be with you. Ask the children to think of times when they have met assertive behaviour and how they reacted to it.

Activity sheet

Make sure that the children know the stories on this activity sheet. You may also have to talk about some TV programmes with assertive characters in them.

Assertiveness   My name is......................

Write whether you think these story book characters were assertive or not. What would you say to them?

I think Cinderella was............................. I would have said: 'Hey Cinders...

I think Goldilocks was........................ I would have said, 'Really Goldilocks,

I think the smallest Billy Goat Gruff was.............................I would have said, 'Hey Little Billy, ...

I think Big Billy goat gruff was .... I would have said, 'Billy...

Think about an assertive character in a TV programme and write about an incident that showed them being assertive.

Turn over the paper.

Think about your own assertiveness and write about occasions when you were not assertive enough and one where you were. What were the outcomes?

Self-belief

Ideal self

Ask the children to think of the kind of person they would like be and way they would like others to see them. Ask them to volunteer words and phrases to give a profile of the person they would like to be viewed as; explain that this is not about appearance, but personality or character. List the qualities they say their ideal self would have and discuss these.

> **I'd like people to see me as…**
> thoughtful
> kind
> helpful
> confident
> self-assured
> cooperative
> caring
> supportive
> dependable
> honest
> trustworthy
> sympathetic.

How I think someone sees me

Ask the children to think of how other people might view them. Ask them to think of people in their family and friends at school and how these people might see them. Ask them to choose just one very supportive and loving person and to write down a few sentences of how they think that this person views them with examples of why they think this. Ask them to write whether they think they can live up to this person's expectations.

How my friend sees me

Ask the children to work in pairs and each write down a list of the other's good points. Ask them to share their lists with each other and discuss why the partner thinks they have these good points. Come together as a group and ask the children to raise a hand if they were surprised at how their partner sees their good points. Were many of the children surprised?

I see myself

Ask each child to write down first a list of their own good personal qualities and then a list of qualities that they realise are not so good. Why do they think they have these good qualities? Is it because of what people say or a feeling inside themselves? Could some qualities be in both lists? Ask them to look at their 'not so good' list. Some of these may be good qualities in disguise, for example, if they are impatient at times, this quality may help them to get on in the world and not waste time; if they are slow at work, this quality may help them to make sure that their work is of a high quality.

Self-belief

Discuss these sentences.

- With self belief, hard work and perseverance you can achieve anything
- Knowing your strengths and weakness will help you to achieve.

Ask children to research well known people who have had to overcome problems or disability to succeed.

Activity sheet

Children focus on their ideal self and how others see them. They are asked to list their strengths and to identify one thing they want to be able to do and how to go about this.

Self-belief

My name is..........................

My ideal self is...

I think my grown-ups at home see me as a person who is good at ...

I think my friends see me as a person who is good at...

I think my teachers see me as a person who is good at...

I know these are my strengths...

Turn over the paper.

Write one thing that you want to be able to do or to be. List the steps in learning to do or be this. Write down how you will go about learning to do this thing. Write a statement of positive intent, which starts, 'I believe that I can...

Strengths

Talk to the children about knowing their own strengths. Remind them that we all have strengths and that they must recognise their own and use these to help them to feel more confident. Talk about the kinds of strengths you mean, for example, things we are good at and things we enjoy doing as well as skills.

My strengths

Ask each child to write a private list of their own strengths and keep this privately at home. Perhaps they can display it on the wall in their bedroom and add to the list something that they want to improve so that they can add this to their strengths list.

> **My strengths**
>
> good at reading
> like small children
> enjoy most sports
> do neat writing
> good at table tennis
> like to help at home
> flexible in PE
> can draw cartoons
> am usually happy
> lots of friends.

Your strengths

Ask the children to work in pairs and each to write down what they think are the strengths of their partner. Ask them to share their list with their partner and discuss how each of them feels about the lists of strengths. Are they surprised or pleased? Has their partner found a strength in them that they didn't know they possessed? Ask them to add these strengths to the list they have at home.

Personal skills

Ask the children to focus on the skills they possess. As well as things they are good at and things they are learning to get better at, there are other skills of personality, such as, for example, the skill of maintaining friendships, having empathy, caring for others, helping people, excusing others, seeing the best in people and so on. Ask them to help you to make a list. Read through the list they helped to make and ask them to think hard to see if they can add any of these personal skills to their own list of strengths.

Vicious circles: positive

Explain to the children that if they use their strengths they will feel good about themselves and this will help them to learn new skills more easily. Ask them to think of this as a circle, with the positive skills producing more positive actions. Remind them of the wheel of success in the 'Feeling good' section. Give them this example; you enjoy swimming, you practise and get better, someone praises you, you feel good and enjoy swimming even more. Ask the children to work in pairs to draw out a circle of increasing positivity, using a strength one of them has as the starting point. Try this with other strengths.

Vicious circles: negative

Now ask them to work alone and make a negative circle. Can they see how being negative can stop them from feeling confident and succeeding?

Activity sheet

Remind the children about letter writing, how to set out the address and date. They may like to write the letter in rough first.

Strengths

My name is..

Write a letter to a new pen-pal. You'll need to tell them all about yourself so make sure you include all your strengths at home and at school. Don't forget your address at the top and the date. Make sure you end your letter well.

Dear pen-pal,

Turn over the paper.

Think of all the people you know, your family and friends. Choose four of them and write down their strengths. Write about how you feel when you are with these people. Does their confidence help you to feel more or less confident yourself? What do you do about this?

Control

Talk to the children about the meaning of being in control when you are taking responsibility for something or someone. Ask them to finish the sentence: 'I was in control when…' Discuss each one and celebrate the children's ability to be in charge.

I was in control when my mum went shopping and I had to wait in on my own for a delivery.

How did you feel?

Explore how we feel when we are left in charge or take responsibility for something. Does it make us feel worried by this responsibility or do we feel happy to be allowed to take control? Ask the children to consider this scenario:

You are left in charge of a 5th birthday party for your sister at your house with ten children playing in the garden. Your parents are in the house having a breather.

Ask the children:

- How could you plan for this?
- What kinds of things would you do?
- How would you feel taking this responsibility?
- How would you feel when it was all over?

Ask the children to put a thumb up if they would feel good about this ask to put a thumb down if they would not like this responsibility. Discuss their reasons.

Control of feelings

Explain to the children the concept of being in control of their feelings and not letting their feelings control their actions. Explain that those who are confident, with high self-esteem, will be able to control their feelings and not let themselves get out of control. Ask the children to write about an occasion when they were able to control their feelings and what the outcome was. Ask them to reflect on this situation and write what could have happened if they had lost control.

Losing control

Remind the children that nothing is gained by losing control and ask them to work in small groups and write down a list of things they can do to keep control, for example, take a deep breath, count to ten… Make a list of these ways of keeping control and talk about the efficacy of each one. Do some strategies work better in various situations? Can the children pin situations to the 'keeping control' strategies? Ask the groups to make a list of occasions when they might possibly lose control and write alongside each one the best keeping control strategies.

Activity sheet

Talk about the taking of responsibility and being in control as something they will have to get used to as they get older and move to their next school.

Control   My name is.............................

What do these people control? Write down their responsibility

The school crossing patrol

The person who delivers your mail

The bank manager

The swimming instructor

The football coach

The street sweeper

The householders

Write about your responsibilities as a family member. Are you in control of anything?

What are your responsibilities as a learner at your school?

What will your responsibilities be when you move to your next school and how will you feel about them?

Turn over the paper.

Write about how you control your feelings; include times and places when you need to keep in good control, how you do this, how you feel if you lose control, what you do then, who helps you to regain control and how you make yourself feel better about it.

APPENDIX

Certificate of Attendance

This certificate is awarded by

....school

to

....

for

**attending all the
Self-Esteem Workshops**

In the .... *term,* .....

Self-esteem profile

I feel good about myself.
I am happy with myself just as I am.
I make friends easily and enjoy being with them.
I deserve people to love and respect me.
I feel valued.
I can speak up for myself.
I never worry about what other people think of me.
I am (nearly always) in control of my feelings.
When I make a mistake I can admit it and make amends.
If people justly criticise me, I can accept it and try to do better.
I don't think other people are better off than I am.
I don't need approval from other people, but can accept it gracefully.
I enjoy challenges and making decisions.
I am happy to take responsibility within my capabilities.
I understand how other people feel and can see their point of view.

The Optimist Creed

Promise Yourself

To be so strong that nothing can disturb your peace of mind.

To talk health, happiness and prosperity to every person you meet.

To make all your friends feel that there is something in them.

To look at the sunny side of everything and make your optimism come true.

To think only of the best, to work only for the best, and to expect only the best.

To be just as enthusiastic about the success of others as you are about your own.

To forget the mistakes of the past and press on to the greater achievements of the future.

To wear a cheerful countenance at all times and give every living creature you meet a smile.

To give so much time to the improvement of yourself that you have no time to criticize others.

To be too large for worry, too noble for anger, too strong for fear, and too happy to permit the presence of trouble.

Reproduced here with kind permission of:

Dana L. Thomas

Executive Assistant

Optimist International

4494 Lindell Blvd

St. Louis MO 63108 USA

800.500.8130 x 201

dana.thomas@optimist.org

who says that 'The Optimist Creed is public domain – you may use it freely'.

Resources

Self-esteem further reading

Margaret Collins, *Because We're Worth It: Enhancing Self-Esteem in Young Children* (2001)

Margaret Collins, *Circle Time for the Very Young*, Second Edition (2007)

Denis Lawrence, *Enhancing Self-esteem in the Classroom*, Third Edition (2006)

Barbara Quartey & Tina Rae, *Developing Parenting Skills, Confidence and Self-Esteem: A Training Programme* (2001)

Tina Rae et al, *Developing Emotional Literacy with Teenage Girls: Developing Confidence, Self-Esteem and Self-Respect* (2005)

Tina Rae, *Confidence, Assertiveness, Self-Esteem: A Series of 12 Sessions for Secondary School Students* (2000)

Rosemary Roberts, *Self-Esteem and Early Learning: Key People from Birth to School* (2006)

Yvonne Weatherhead, *Creative Circle Time Lessons for the Early Years* (2008)

Murray White, *Magic Circles: Self-Esteem for Everyone in Circle Time*, Second Edition (2008)